IAN McNAMARA

AUSTRALIA ALL OVER

an ABC BOOK

Published by ABC Enterprises for the
AUSTRALIAN BROADCASTING CORPORATION
GPO Box 9994 Sydney NSW 2001

National Library of Australia
Cataloguing-in-Publication entry
McNamara, Ian
    Australia all over.

    ISBN 0 7333 0252 1.

    1. Australia—Social life and customs. 2. Australia—Social
    conditions. I. Australian Broadcasting Corporation. 2. Title.
    III. Title: Australia all over (Radio program).
994

Illustrated and designed by Helen Semmler
Set in 11/14 Berkeley Old Style by Midland Typesetters,
    Maryborough, Victoria
Film by Litho Platemakers, Adelaide
Printed and bound in Australia by
    Australian Print Group, Maryborough
    Victoria

30SP, 20APG

FOR THE PEOPLE

ACKNOWLEDGMENTS

My sincere thanks to those who helped put this book together: Virginia Love and Peter Walsh from *Australia All Over* for patiently extracting possible material from a mountain of letters and tapes; Sally Milner for publishing skills when guiding the shape of the book; Dawn Webb for editorial input; Helen Semmler for designing a radio program into a book; Andrew Rankin for, as ever, an excellent cover photograph.

CONTENTS

INTRODUCTION

BY IAN McNAMARA

I never wanted to compere *Australia All Over* and, come to think of it, I was never actually offered the job! I think, at the time, nobody else wanted it. It was 1981 and Mike Broadhurst, who compered it then, was going on long service leave. He said to me, 'Do you want to do the program?', and in my usual style I said, 'Oh, no, I don't think I could do it', or words to that effect.

Anyway, I did a pilot program and there I was. In those days the program was described as a 'Radio Three program for country people', which meant that it was broadcast only in rural Australia (except for Western Australia) from seven o'clock till a quarter to ten on Sunday mornings, and the whole thing was pre-recorded on Thursday afternoons.

Prior to first compering the program in October 1981, I was the producer or, more accurately, the 'minder' for Mike Broadhurst. Each Thursday afternoon, armed with a big suitcase full of records and tapes and bits and pieces, we'd wend our way to the studio to spend three hours pre-recording *Australia All Over*. It was a great learning experience because I could watch someone doing the program and learn what to do and what not to do. For three years I was learning the nuts and bolts.

And being in the ABC was a great learning experience. Since I started there in 1976 I'd done a lot of things, including working on television programs like *A Big Country* and *Countrywide*. But, above all, I loved radio.

When I finished my University degree I decided not to go on with economics and took a course in radio instead. I found it as exciting as I had at school, when my sister and I used to go into Sydney's 2UW after school to a radio show called *Rumpus Room* and answer questions and read ads on the air. That was really exciting, but I was only allowed to go when my big sister took me into town! I wanted to work as a sports broadcaster—I suppose after Richie Benaud declined to include me in the Australian cricket team! Anyway, I finally joined the ABC, not in radio but in the Finance and Industrial Relations Departments and, after two years of trying, started to work in radio. By that time I knew enough about it to keep my head above water, and I got to stay.

If *Australia All Over* had been anything other than a Sunday morning program in a forgotten timeslot at some ungodly hour I wouldn't have been doing it. But no-one seemed to want to broadcast to the country on Sunday morning or, rather, on Thursday afternoon for Sunday morning. It seemed a totally unattractive program and an unattractive timeslot—but not to me.

So I pre-recorded the program from 1981 to the middle of 1984, and then I went to another job in current affairs for about a year. My return to *Australia All Over* at the start of 1986 coincided with a change in timeslot and style. It became a live program and I just knew that it was right for all Australians, not just for country people: that the things we talked about were applicable to city and country dwellers alike. So, in a polite, positive way I began to investigate the possibility of being heard on metropolitan stations, and I think the reason the program finally got onto the metropolitan networks was that the Australian people put it there. They wanted to hear it. No enlightened decisions put *Australia All Over* into the cities. Once it started to be heard on a part-time basis in Sydney, Newcastle, Canberra and, I think, Hobart, the other states followed. Now it is heard nationwide.

What makes *Australia All Over* the most popular radio program in Australia's history, as the ABC's Managing Director, David Hill, describes it? Many things, among them the fact that it's a national program that all Australians feel part of; the fact that it's 'fair dinkum'. It doesn't sound pretentious, I hope— what you hear is what you get. There's a down-to-earth humour about it. It's not precious, and seeks to give everybody a go.

I think one of the nicest things to have happened on the program was the McNamara Cultural Society, formed in Werribee, Victoria, by Barry Armstrong and Tom Toohey, purely because at that stage—1988 or 1989— they couldn't hear the program in Melbourne. They heard it and enjoyed it when they went out in the bush, which a lot of city people do, and wondered why they couldn't hear it when they got back to the city. One bloke regularly drove to the Dandenongs in Victoria to listen because he couldn't hear it in Melbourne!

More and more over recent times, certainly in the last two or three years, we've been getting calls from all over the world as Australians travel further afield. They ring up on Sunday mornings from Japan, the Netherlands, the United States, navy boats on exercises in the oceans of the world, soldiers with peace-keeping forces in Cambodia.

Then there's the story behind *Over the Top with Jim*. Mrs Jenny Newsham sent me the book and said, 'You'll enjoy this. When you finish it, pass it on to David Hill'—which I haven't done! I enjoyed the book very much and Australians just loved the whole package—Hugh Lunn's book, Peter Curtin's reading, and the music that went with it. But if Jenny Newsham hadn't written to me there would have been no *Over the Top with Jim* on *Australia All Over*. Of course, without Hugh Lunn there would have been no book. Hugh is a great chronicler of an Australia that many of us can relate to. What a wonderful book he's written! Many of our books, music and television programs still come from America and Britain; Hugh's book is a triumph for Australian publishing.

The most enjoyable thing I do apart from the program is play music. I love being part of a band, singing harmonies. The concerts that I do occasionally are most enjoyable. I'd love to play in a little nightclub or restaurant somewhere. Ours was a musical family. My Dad played the trombone and my Mum played the bagpipes. Actually, as I told a listener one morning, they used to walk around the house playing duets—imagine that, if you can!

Music has been an integral part of the success of *Australia All Over*. Songs like 'I Made a Hundred in the Backyard at Mum's', 'Gumboots', and 'G'day, G'day' have probably helped the revival of Australian music, which is a great thing. I write some of the music for the program myself: 'Over the Top with Jim' and 'A Hundred Tons of Washing', written especially for the people of Nyngan, are a couple of examples.

A question people always ask me is, 'What do you do for the rest of the week?' I just smile and think, if you only knew! Well, I'll try to explain.

On Sunday, of course, I do the program, usually from a studio in Sydney but fairly often while travelling to various parts of Australia. In a normal week there are interviews to do, tapes to edit, promos to cut, serials to record and edit, music to find and record, mail to read and answer—there are just not enough hours in the week, and that's why I find myself working seven days. As well as this there's reading books and magazines and looking for books and stories. Did I mention travelling, meeting people, doing record albums, and so on?

I'm not the kind of person who likes to sit still for too long, but when I get a chance I've been enjoying learning the trombone for the last two or three years. It's continually frustrating because to learn any musical instrument you really need to play it every day for an hour or two, but after spending twelve hours or so at work I'm just too tired to practise.

Most of the ideas for the program either come from listeners or from me talking to people. I try to steer away from newspapers. And I reckon

Australia All Over has the best stories of all. One thing I've noticed over the last four or five years is that the program has helped millions of Australians rediscover the environment and our flora and fauna. It's nice for Australians to get to know and like their trees and birds, because if they do there's a good chance that they'll help save them. I don't have to tell you how much our plants and animals are under threat.

I always try to make the program and its music fresh and original, but its real essence is the people who are part of it. Try this for a blend: Father Chris Power from New Norcia; the lady who rang up and said she listens to earthquakes and atomic bombs on Sunday morning; the bloke who caught a crocodile in his crab pots overnight and offered it in exchange for Peter Allen's maracas; the bloke who lived in a caravan park in Rockhampton who, when I played 'Ain't Misbehavin'' one Sunday morning, asked me to yell out the chords so that he could write them down (he was learning guitar); Warwick Tainton, a Qantas pilot, flying back from Singapore; and Peter Burge, the great Test cricketer from the '50s and '60s who wanted to talk about backyard cricket.

Ordinary Australians from all races and walks of life contribute to the program by phone and by letter. They write great letters—you'll read many of them in this book. I know the politicians listen, too, because they write to me and say they can get a handle on Australia, on what Australians are thinking. Although we're not a current affairs program the issues canvassed in *Australia All Over* are the real issues that concern Australians. I don't start these debates. They're started by the listeners—the callers and letter writers. I'm just the editor, I suppose. I don't often read letters that criticise, mainly because I like the program to remain positive It attracts criticism, of course, both inside and outside the ABC, but my mother once told me not to listen to either praise or criticism—pretty good advice, too, I think.

The people I've talked to most often about the program and, in fact, about life, are my parents—my Mum and, while he was alive, my father. They were great influences on me—very sensible and clever people. In fact, that's what I base the program on. I think about my clever parents and their families: our uncles and aunties and grandfathers and grandmothers, ordinary Australians who read many books and could do lots of things, and I know that there are millions of Australians out there who are just like them but are never heard of. The vast repository of the wealth of Australia is in its people, and you can hear them every Sunday morning. They are just wonderful, great and clever, and that's why Australia's an outstanding country.

Sunday mornings can be pretty chaotic, of course. Sometimes when you've got a program prepared it all goes haywire because a phone call will start something off and it flies off on a tangent. But that's the best part of the program and what I enjoy. It's not pre-scripted, it's really off the cuff. We get literally hundreds of phone calls every Sunday morning and it's a pretty stressful juggling act to try to get it all to air. But it's very satisfying if at ten o'clock you can look back and say, 'Well, that was a bloody good program!'.

And don't the people who ring in have vim and vigour? Well, mostly, anyway! They're so vital—like Mary from Gulgong, Gilbert from Tweed Heads and Herbert Price from Rocky. I always find them interesting. Very occasionally it's hard to get a caller off the line, but more often than not it's the good humour and the helpful nature of Australians that shine through.

One of the things I like to do is 'go on the road' away from the cities and take *Australia All Over* all over. And one of the most challenging things I do is to take the program live out into a park or into a hall, in front of a live audience. It's great fun, but very draining, and requires a lot of coordination and a good support staff. The ones we've done—Melbourne in the park, Toowoomba in the Carnival of Flowers, Brisbane in the park and Rockhampton at the railway station—were a great success. We get big crowds of a couple of thousand people and I get to meet the listeners and they get to meet me.

My love for the bush came from the time I spent as a young bloke on my uncle's sheep property. I liked the space. And I had a grandfather who used to recite poetry about the bush and talk to me about it. I believe Australia's heart and soul are in the bush. There are cities like Melbourne and Sydney all over the world, but our trees and landscape are unique. Australia is probably the only place in the world where you can still see the stars and blue skies most of the time. And, of course, our Aborigines have offered us their unique heritage to share, and on Sunday mornings I try to give people a sense of this important aspect of Australian life.

I suppose you can gauge that I'm pretty proud to be a part of *Australia All Over*. I love doing the program and think it's the best in Australia, bar none. It's certainly the most listened to, and the reason is that I've got millions of reporters tuning in every Sunday morning. You can't beat it. They are the stars of the program.

I like a bit of a laugh on *Australia All Over*. That's mostly, I think, why the program makes you smile. But sometimes, like all of us, I get cranky, especially about the Americanisation of our culture, a lot of our commercial television and our football teams. Some Rugby League teams choose American names: the latest ones I've heard are the Perth Pumas and the North Queensland Cowboys—can you believe it? Why do we want to be American clones? The best things in Australia, the highest rating things, are Australian—like the Hogan shows and, of course, *Australia All Over*. Why? Because they're Australian and good. I rarely watch television now.

I think it's really important for our children, too, to get out and learn about life and nature and do things with their own hands. Hugh Lunn tells a story about going to schools and asking the children, 'Now, who do you think had the best childhood—you or me?'. They all put up their hands and say, 'You did. Mr Lunn!' And he says, 'Why?' 'Because you did really fun things like making slingshots and canoes and stuff like that.' 'Well, why don't you do that?' They say things like, 'We're not allowed to', or 'We watch TV', or 'We play video games.'

This book represents only a fraction of the letters and phone calls that come in to *Australia All Over*. You simply couldn't put all the information that I get into one book—it just wouldn't fit! Anyway, read it from camp to camp, and I hope you enjoy it.

Finally, I think the program is summed up perfectly in this quote from Warwick Frank of Bathurst, New South Wales, in the academic magazine *Rural Society*:

> '*Australia All Over* represents a celebration and reaffirmation of a traditional view of the essence of Australia, but within this approach there are persistent notes of questioning, revision and scepticism which give the program a richness and depth.'

BIRDS

Some pretty funny things happen on *Australia All Over* from time to time. Probably the funniest was when Arthur Dean from Dimboola wrote about the Orpington chook; after that I got letters from all over the place. The one from Martin Fitzgerald of Narrogin really cracked me up, and there were many other good ones, too.

As far as birds go, *Australia All Over* is a little bit like Neighbourhood Watch. People write and report bird behaviour of all sorts, from currawongs to crows. And magpies. Magpies!!! Do me a favour! The magpie must be Australia's most observed bird.

Everybody seems to be interested in birds. And why not? They are the cleverest creatures, original Aussies, with great songs. The bird call tape that I play on the program is endlessly popular.

As I was reading and selecting the letters and poems to include in this book I realised just how marvellous they are. There are some great ones in this chapter, particularly Dorothy Watt's 'The Lament of the Lyrebird'.

FROM:
ARTHUR DEAN
Dimboola
Victoria

I'm writing to tell you this experience my sister and I had going back about forty-five years ago. We were going to a tin-banging for a couple just married—they had those functions those days.

Well, we were going to drive in the buggy and, as the chooks roosted on the buggies in the shed, we hunted them all off and away we went. We arrived at the place and tied the horses up to the fence and were just walking away and happened to look back, and to our amazement there was an old black Orpington chook sitting on the back axle. I might mention that we drove a distance of about three-and-a-half miles over rough roads and gave the horses a crack with the whip a few times which caused them to go off with a jerk. It was almost a miracle that she stayed there all that way. We decided that we would leave her there, but she fell off somewhere on the way home. Never heard what happened to her—probably a fox got her.

FROM:
MARTIN FITZGERALD
Narrogin

Western Australia

Where the chook (Bess the Black Orpington) is now, I don't know, but your story explained something that I saw one morning by the Mukinbudin—Bullfinch Road, somewhere between Warralakin and Boodarocking, a few years ago.

We were both pretty sleepy and just poking along letting the engine warm up, with early sun right in our eyes, when the old man said in a quiet mumble, 'That'd be the worst rolled swag I ever saw'.

I thought the poor old bugger was talking in his sleep and looked over at him, but his eyes were open. Well, as open as mine anyway, and I said 'What?'

'That chook. You nearly ran over it.'

'Chook?' I said.

'Struth, I must be going right off. But I saw it. A chook, with a little swag on its back and its feet wrapped in rag.'

We were hardly travelling at all so the argument only took about half a mile before I swore I'd go back and have him show me the chook or have him certified.

Well, we went back and I was showing him the vacant open road with the sun behind us and wondering how bad he'd get before we got back to our own country. He kept on mumbling, and then pointed away from the road, down one of those little well-worn pads shared by 'roos and sheep probably, but you never see anything actually use them. Out there, moving up a little rise, was something, sure enough. It went over the rise and I jumped in and drove to find out what it was.

Well, we caught up to it. A Black Orpington, or what was left of the poor scrawny beggar.

'Poor little sod,' said the old man, 'no wonder that swag looks so bad. He ain't got the shoulders for this game'.

'She, I think Pop, but it don't make much difference. I wonder where it got the little pieces of blue jeans to wrap its feet?'

We tried talking to the chook, feeling a bit silly, but all we could get back as it plodded wearily away was, 'Arthur, Arthur'. Well that explains it. I'd been wondering who Arthur was.

I have listened with interest over the past two weeks about the black Orpington hen from Dimboola. She was certainly not killed on the way home from the 'tin-bash', and the two motorists from Western Australia were partly right when they said 'she hasn't the shoulders for it'. She didn't, but she eventually worked out how to carry her swag effectively, nesting it on the broad of her back, with the string ends tied just below her neck.

FROM:
PHILLIP RUSH
Sarsfield
Victoria

I had the pleasure of meeting her a number of times, the last being just north of Bucham in East Gippsland in 1959. The attached poem tells as much about 'Bess'—that was what she called herself as I know, but I'm sure your listeners would have a lot more to add.

Bess The Orpington Swaggie
by Phillip Rush

She was raised on a farm in Dimboola
surrounded by Wimmera wheat
she knew icy frosts in the winter,
she suffered the long summer's heat
a little black Orpington chicken
she grew to a good laying hen
but her thoughts often turned to adventure,
away from a wire netting pen.

Each morning the farmer's son Arthur
would let her out into the yard
along with the rest of the layers
for whom she had little regard.
For Bess, as this Arthur had named her,
was a tough independent young chook
and she'd spend many hours gazing westwards
with a dreamy far away look.

My future is not as a layer
I'm sure there are more sights to see,
than I could ever imagine

and the life on the road is for me.
So she gathered a few basic items,
wrapped up in a calico bag
and tied the bag up in a blanket
a little black Orpington swag.

Thereafter each night she would settle
not in with the rest of the hens
but under the cart on the axle
for this was a means to her ends.
At last came the night she was waiting
the family went out in the cart
and she humped along on the axle
excitement rose high in her heart.

The family was off to tin-kettle
a young couple who'd recently wed
and they waited, of course, till they reckoned
the couple would be well in bed.
So off in the darkness they trotted
unaware that black Bess underneath

was having a ride, had she had them,
that would loosen all of her teeth.

So the couple was duly tin-kettled
then Arthur discovered the hen
'Hey look!' he exclaimed most astonished
Black Bess has got out of her pen.
Twas then that Black Bess nearly panicked
but she kept her swag hidden from view
and Arthur said, 'Might as well leave her
she looks like she's stuck on with glue!'

When they'd finished tin kettling the couple
they all drifted back to their homes:
the Gardeners, the Smiths, and the Griffiths,
the Shepherds, the Menzies, the Baums.
But Black Bess never reached the old farmhouse
she jumped off at the road heading west
with a swag, with its blankets and billy
she started her journey with zest.

Through the small hours of morning she plodded
and then right on break of day
they saw her nearing Japarrot
two travellers from over Perth way.
No longer a jaunty young chicken
her feet were now blistered and raw
and she'd wrapped them up in blue denim
to stop them feeling so sore.

One of the travellers stopped her
and spoke with a voice kind and true
And what are you doing young chicky,
and where are you travelling to?'
But Bessie could not speak too clearly
and the one word that she answered back
was a feebly drawn out, husky, 'AAArthur'
as she stumbled along on the track.

There was drought in the wheatbelt that summer
and meals were a problem each day
but she worked her way all round the country
from Quilpie to Wentworth and Hay.
She swept up the crutchings in woolsheds
she helped press the wool in the bales

she even helped out with a muster
way out in west NSW.

She tramped through the year '47
the year of the Mallee mouse plague
she remembered it all very clearly
though my recollections are vague.
She ate rabbit stew with the swaggies
and often repaid with an egg
for an Orpington proud was young Bessie
she'd vowed she'd not steal food or beg.

After two or three years in the outback
she headed for different terrain
it was up in the mountains I met her
with the cattle up on the high plain.
She told me she'd often missed Arthur
to Dimboola one day she'd return
but she still had her sense of adventure
she still had a lot more to learn.

By now she was really quite famous
Black Bess the Orpington chook
and the shearers and drovers all knew her
she was often employed as their cook.
She'd learnt to play fiddle and banjo
and many a station outback
would ask her to play at their dances
each time she blew in from the track.

She travelled from Wave Hill to Derby
and then on to Kimberley Downs
she travelled all over Australia
keeping out of the really big towns.
For some years I heard nothing of her
I thought she by then must've died
but late in the fifties I saw her
there was no mistaking her stride.

I pulled up beside her and chatted,
and strike me she called me by name
this now battered old graying Bessie
still plucky, courageous and game.
She still had her bluey and billy
the same that she'd taken that day

from the kitchen she'd known as a chicken
when she lived over Dimboola way.

She said with a voice sounding weary
she'd now had enough of the track
with the flies and the dust and the tourists
too many now travel outback.
She said that she'd do one more circuit
to say fond goodbyes to her friends
then settle back home in Dimboola
with Arthur and some of the hens.

And so we're in 1990
I've not seen old Bess now for years
but sometimes when old timers are chatting

I a rumour occasionally hears
about a Black Orpington swaggie
they'd met somewhere out on the track
but I doubt that I'll ever again see her
I doubt that she'll ever come back.

So Arthur, I heard of your letter
on *Australia All Over* you said
that you'd last seen young Bess at a tin bash
she never returned to the shed.
But Arthur, I hope you are listening
your Bess was a dinkum true blue
and intended, when her journeys were over
to come back to Dimboola and you.

I was amazed to say the least when I heard you reading a letter regarding the couple who went to the tin-bash.

I myself was travelling that particular road on that very same night when lo and behold I came across this rather grand looking chook; it was moving but only just. This is what caught my eye on this very dark night. I thought I had better hop out and check it out, which I did. Alas, I was unable to identify it with any particular farmer around this area, otherwise I would have searched them out to tell them that the poor old chook was dead in fact, BRAIN DEAD. A puncture hole revealed itself on the top of the head. I thought to myself, now this looks like a nail hole which could have been protruding from a buggy base board just above the axle which must have been bouncing along at a great speed to have caused this vile injury.

I buried this elegant creature at the roadside site where it would be seen some forty to forty-five years ago. I was truly delighted when I heard you read that letter cos' now I can return and mark that grave. I have seen these graveyards all over the country side and have assumed that they are in memory of the same chook.

After hearing the problems your apiarist mate had with Rainbow Birds, or Bee-Eaters, I thought I might contribute something about them.

I feel sorry for him and other bee-keepers because they can clean up a hive of bees in no time flat, but such a beautiful and tenacious bird deserves a bit of help, and I think they're diminishing.

Their colouring defies description—almost as beautiful as our Gouldian

Finch—and to see them banking and wheeling in the spring sunshine while catching insects on the wing is something to behold!

They migrate here from south-east Asia each October, (same time as the Dollar Bird) and that's no mean feat for a small bird.

They mate, nest, rear their young and depart for south-east Asia late March or April.

The nest is interesting as they dig a tunnel, like Kingfishers, in the sandy bank of a gully or creek, or sometimes nest in a hollow tree, and I've even seen them dig a nest in the raised ridge between two wheel tracks on a sandy back road.

Over the past thirty years, we've spent a lot of time near Yuragin National Park on the north coast of NSW, and have spent many hours watching hundreds and hundreds of Rainbow Birds where they once came in numbers.

Banjo Paterson wrote a beaut little piece in 1933 which paid tribute to these birds; it's called 'Why The Jackass Laughs' and was published in a collection of Paterson's poems under the heading, 'The Animals Noah Forgot'. Norman Lindsay did the illustrations when he and Paterson both worked for *The Bulletin*.

FROM:
JOHN PORTER
Berrimah
Northern Territory

Yesterday I caught the tail end of a story about a meeting of crows on your program.

In 1950 I was at Gunningbar Station. near Nevertire NSW for the shearing. It had to be delayed because of the flood and we were stranded there. One day the manager and I went out on horseback and heard this row we couldn't identify. A very large dead tree was covered with hundreds of crows. The noise was frightening. The horses were out of condition and very tired, but still took some hanging on to. One crow would 'kark' very loudly, others would interject and sometimes all of them would jump about and 'kark' madly. We were glad to leave them.

I've told about this in most parts of Australia and never heard of anything like it.

As a sideline, one of the reasons we rode out was to see how the manager's rabbit control methods were succeeding. They weren't. There were rabbits on every bit of dry land—rabbits on logs, rabbits way up in trees, rabbits swimming.

And we thought the place was well under control!

FROM:
BILL
YATES
Chermside
West, Qld.

I was particularly interested in your segment regarding magpies and also your comments about the old mature trees being lost as nesting

12

sites for birds and that it will take many years for hollows to be formed in the billions of young trees to be planted.

I live in the suburb of Chermside West in Brisbane, close to Huxtable Park, which is 10.5 hectares in area and is looked after by a neighbourhood group called the Neighbours of Huxtable Park. In years gone by in the name of development and progress many of the older trees were removed. However, there are still some solid old specimens of bloodwood, tallowwood and the gum remaining which provide nesting sites for galahs, possums, rainbow lorikeets and rosellas.

To overcome the shortage of natural hollows the Neighbours have placed artificial nest boxes in many of the trees. Already many of the boxes have been used by the birds to raise their young. These artificial nest boxes have proved so popular with our 'feathered friends' that some species have taken up residence within twelve hours of the box being installed.

The Neighbours of Huxtable Park are a voluntary self-funded group of residents who maintain Huxtable Park. In the last five years they have planted over 1000 native trees, do their own fund raising, mowing, watering, install seats, signs and general maintenance. This year over 2000 man hours will be spent in improving the park.

P.S. Our new magpie warning sign is soon to be installed. Our magpies up here are more lethal than B52 bombers.

As a retired bloke, I cycle a lot, and have only been approached by the NWM (Neighbourhood Watch Magpie) when I forget to protect myself against sun cancer by not wearing a hat. His obvious concern for my welfare has prompted me to wear a hat at all times and to reciprocate by providing tucker on demand for any magpie at my back door. An agreement which seems to suit both parties.

P.S. Love your show (as well as birds).

FROM: DAVE GIBBONS
Canberra, ACT

The problems experienced by various people during the annual magpie nesting season, not to mention the innumerable, and often pointless, means put forward as being solutions to the problem, never cease to intrigue me.

As country schoolboys in the late 'thirties, we were taught that a magpie who trusted you never attacked, and we were encouraged to feed them to establish this trust.

Magpies habitually nested in a tree in a paddock adjoining the school ground, and we would bring small amounts of mincemeat, wrapped in grease-proof paper, as an offering to the hard-worked parent birds, in

FROM: GARRY J. MAIDEN
Brighton
Queensland

exchange for which we would then be permitted to play, immune from attack, in the immediate area.

Of notable exception was the treatment handed out by the birds to one boy who, I suspect, must have molested the birds at some time or other, and for which misdemeanour they never saw fit to forgive, or forget!

Primo's route, to and from school, lay across the said paddock, and, during nesting season, traverse of this area became a running of the gauntlet for him.

His twice-daily, four-minute-mile sprint, school bag clutched tightly across the top of his head and hotly pursued by the two black and white terrorists, was a delight to the more sadistic of us, and the tactics used by the birds to counter Primo's defensive efforts would have done credit to any Battle of Britain pilot!

Primo wore a hair style which became known in later years as a crew-cut, and which left little or no defence against the beak of a determined magpie, so a favourite tactic was a low beam attack by one bird. This would result in the panic-stricken Primo flailing with his school bag and thus momentarily leaving his scalp vulnerable to a diving attack from the other bird positioned nicely above him, an attack which was unfailingly delivered with speed and accuracy!

I was most interested to hear your magpie expert last week. I live at Seven Mile Beach in southern Tasmania amidst masses of magpies—my favourite bird. I would like to know why, at this time of the year lasting for a couple of months, the magpies sing for a lot of the night? Seriously—they do! My bedroom is about thirty metres from a massive gum and at any time I may awake during the night I hear the quiet, lilting warbling, obviously the sub-song the expert spoke of and very similar to his imitation. I have been wondering for years about the magpies singing at night—could your expert give an explanation?

FROM:
ROBYN TROUSSELOT
Seven Mile Beach
Tasmania

I thought you would like this story.

Some years ago we were having a holiday on a sheep property. The property Woltana adjoins Arkaroola owned by Reg Sprig and his son (this is by way of location).

One day Tony was out in the fields and saw a baby magpie, brought him home, and the family hand fed him. Eventually he grew and would fly around the house (as country houses have a verandah all around) about three feet from the ground, and if you were talking to someone he would land on your shoulder and you could not hear yourself talking.

FROM:
BRIAN & MADGE WOOLLEY
Balmoral Beach, NSW

He would play with the cats. On one occasion he was scratching the cat's ear, then stopped. The cat pushed his head up for more. One day one cat who had three kittens was lying down, the kittens were feeding and maggie came along and tried to have a feed with the kittens. Mum cat finally got up and walked off.

Sometime last year while I was working my vegie patch and listening to the music of the morning magpie in the gumtree, I was wondering what simile to use to describe their song. Then an Englishwoman phoned you to relate her new-arrival-impressions of Australia, more particularly the strange noise which she found out belonged to the magpie.

She went on: 'Having lived next to a railway yard back in England, I could only describe what I heard as squeaky railway carriages being shunted.'

Ian, her description fitted beautifully.

It will soon be the time of year when young magpies will be curiously pecking any object on the ground that attracts attention.

The ring from a plastic milk bottle can be a deadly killer to young maggies. If pecked lightly on the rim it will fly back on the beak; the bird then lifts its head, the ring slides over the head and round the neck. If the beak is open enough, the ring slides along between the top and lower beak, then behind the head, similar to the 'bit' in a horse's mouth.

It's a disturbing time for the parent bird, unable to feed a young bird with this ring holding onto the beak. It must result in many deaths among the young birds.

Please ask your listeners to be aware of this threat to young birds.

Your lady caller about sunbaking magpies brought back many happy memories of our dear friend 'Bert'. We found him as a fully feathered but unflightworthy youngster and our home was his, till a wretched chicken hawk put an end to his days.

We have a photo to back up the claim that magpies sunbake. 'Bert' would lie on his stomach, wings out, eyes closed and quite still, then he'd wriggle a bit and toast each side in turn. At these times he never appeared to be preening or making any attempt to rid himself of parasites.

We also have a photo of 'Bert' sound asleep on his back inside a hat, but we're not sure just what this denotes!

FROM: PETER SHOOBRIDGE

FROM: ENID McGARVY East Maitland NSW

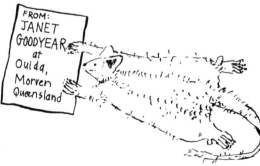

FROM: JANET GOODYEAR at Ouida, Morven Queensland

FROM:
MARY MILSON
Byron Bay
NSW

Just heard you mention magpies singing at night. Many years ago when my husband and I lived on the banks of the Walsh River in North Queensland, we often used to hear butcher birds singing on moonlit nights. What we liked was when they sang in a whisper!

Last year when I was living in a caravan park here in Byron Bay, I shared space and food with a family of butcher birds—pa, ma, teenagers and babies—also a family of magpies. Both lots of birds would sit on my veranda railings or in a tree overhead and hum their songs.

They didn't open their beaks but you could see their throats vibrating—also they would bob their heads as they do when singing 'fortissimo'!

I always felt they were doing it for pleasure and practice, especially the younger birds. Perhaps a little 'thank you' for the food I gave them.

FROM:
FRANK BRADLEY
Alstonville
NSW

In this lovely part of New South Wales we have literally thousands of native trees, and many are in flower at the moment.

We also have (or rather had) many hundreds of rainbow lorikeets until the last couple of weeks, when people began finding dead birds in their gardens.

Under the trees in the school grounds, where the flocks spend the night, the children picked up twenty in one day. According to the local National Parks ranger many people have taken to feeding the birds all sorts of alluring diets based on sugar or jam or honey to attract these troubadours. This is harmful to the birds, as are unclean feeding trays. The best solution is for people to stop feeding the birds altogether.

However, since this is probably not going to happen, you can do this:

1 Only feed proper honeyeater and lorikeet mixture, available from pet shops.
2 Always clean feeding trays and get rid of old food. Don't use terracotta and other earthenware bowls, because these are hard to clean properly.
3 Plant a variety of native flowering shrubs, eg. banksias and grevilleas, in your garden. The birds will use them as a better food source.

All this should stop people killing these beautiful birds with kindness.

FROM:
DENISE CAIN
Mount Isa
Queensland

The blue-winged kookaburra that lives in the top end of Australia doesn't seem to have been very much written about. This is a shy northern relative of the laughing kookaburra. Anything I have read, though, states that the blue-winged is smaller than the laughing kookaburra. We feed blue-winged kookaburras in Mount Isa and have kept track of a family since 1985. These birds are larger than any laughing kookaburras I have seen. I am wondering whether some of your listeners may have noticed the size difference.

I listened enchanted to the lyrebird in your program this morning, hence the following verses. Please ask the gentleman concerned to put the mirror back in the bathroom. The sudden appearances of a rival male lyrebird in his own garden, to say nothing of the equally sudden disappearances, can only lead to unnecessary stress and possible exhaustion for the poor bird, who will, of course, attempt to challenge the intruder and only succeed in damaging himself.

FROM:
DOROTHY WATT
Briagolong
Victoria

The Lament of the Lyrebird

We lyrebirds are the keepers of Australia's history,
Recording through the centuries the forest harmony.
We've filed away the forest sounds in tribal memory
And handed on to each new brood the way things used to be.

We've taught them how to make the sounds
We've listened to for years
And told each chick he must record
Each new sound that he hears.

We've filed the call of every bird
And black men's chanting song
And music made with pipe and stick
To help the dance along.

For generations we've kept faith
And with the greatest care
Recorded all the sounds we heard
On earth and in the air.

But now I think the time has come
To call a lyrebird strike
We've done our best with axe and saw
And engines and the like,

But now we have to draw the line,
Stress levels know no bounds
When we attempt to duplicate
Those electronic sounds

That blare across the forest glades
And through the hidden dells,
Pollute the music of the streams,
Drown tales the wild wind tells.

From raucous box and belching car
And human dancing mound
Comes forth a wild cacophony
Of clashing, jarring sound.

That has no business in the bush
Where peace once reigned supreme
We'll ban it from our repertoire
As it had never been.

So, lyrebirds hatched in times to come
will simply have a blank
Instead of records of this age
In the lyrebird memory bank.

Enclosed are photos of a young magpie 'sun bathing' as some of your listeners discussed.

We have magpies that can be hand fed. Parents are Leigh and Lethal (named after Collingwood coach, Leigh Mathews). The young ones are Bob and Paul (named after you know who).

FROM:
RICHARD TOWNLEY
Camberwell, Victoria

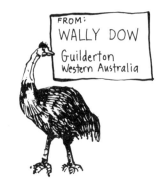

FROM:
WALLY DOW
Guilderton
Western Australia

You have had quite a few stories about magpies. Well, I have a pure white one and it is an albino. It has pink eyes and a pinkish white beak and legs.

Sometimes it is in the utility with me when your show is on, and when that tune comes on with the magpies and other birds he really stacks on a show. When he's in the yard he talks like mad and imitates me. My wife reckons she's quite glad no-one knows what he's saying half the time!

FROM:
PETER DISHER

I have recently returned from an extensive tour of outback Central Australia.

I was appalled to see the number of birds, parrots, mynahs and cockatoos that are being drowned in the water tanks at station bores. I only visited four tanks during my trip, and at two of them there was a heap of feathers and bones where the dead birds had been removed from the tank. At another one there were numerous skulls of birds floating on the surface of the water in the tank. It is obvious that the drowned birds are causing a pollution problem.

It would appear to me that to remedy the situation it would only require a limb of a tree to be placed over the edge of the tank. It would provide a perch for the birds whilst they drank, and if they fell into the water it would provide a means for them to climb out.

It would also solve the water pollution, stop the death of many birds, and save the station owners a lot of time now being used to clean the dead birds from the tanks.

FROM:
COLIN SPRINGALL
Queenscliff
Victoria

Thought you might like to hear a fishing story that I think beats most others. It's how I caught a two pound mullet without a line in the middle of a road!

My wife and I were holidaying at Bargara on the coast out of Bundaberg. We had been for a drive to Elliott Heads and, returning, we were travelling over a causeway at the south end of Kelly's Beach when I noticed a sea eagle (osprey) rising from the water with a large fish grasped tightly in its talons.

It was flying to pass over the causeway and at first I thought it may get in my way. The fish was kicking and the beautiful bird was having trouble gaining altitude. Fortunately we passed, then in my rear view mirror I observed the sea eagle and fish flying across the causeway behind me at rather a low level, probably due to the weight of the fish. Also I noticed that the next vehicle following closely was a large furniture van and I thought he would collect the bird and fish with his radiator.

The fish being so large restricted the height the sea eagle could attain so instead of decorating the radiator of the van it passed between all its wheels. Of course, its wings were restricted and somewhat battered while under the van so it dropped the fish in the middle of the road and flew clear once the van had passed over it. No doubt it was feeling shocked and bruised but really it was lucky to still be able to fly.

At the end of the causeway I did a quick U-turn and returned to pick up the fish which was still very much alive and kicking in the middle of the road.

That evening my wife and I enjoyed a large mullet fillet each for dinner with our thanks to the osprey, as I had left my fishing tackle at home in Queenscliff!

What I want to tell you about is that a couple of weeks ago my wife and I were travelling from Perth to Sydney on the Indian Pacific Train.

We were in the middle of the Nullarbor Plain without a tree or bush as far as the eye could see; even the salt bush had disappeared. We had just finished breakfast when the guard announced over the train's PA system that if we all looked out of the left hand-side of the train we would in a few minutes' time see something wonderful which we would probably never see again and which we would never forget. The train which had been hurtling along at about eighty miles per hour slowed down to a crawl and at the side of the track in one of the telegraph poles was a wedge-tail eagle's nest with two snow-white eagle chicks sitting up in the nest and watching the train. The two parent birds were sitting on the cross bars of the next pole. It was a magnificent sight, one I know I shan't see again, as eagles usually nest in the highest tree they can find. As there aren't any trees out there they have to make do with the rather short telegraph poles along the railway line. I wonder where they get water away out there?

Here in Tasmania the wildlife authorities estimate that there are only seventy pairs of nesting eagles left. This magnificent bird has been poisoned and shot for years. Just before we went on our trip two were found shot and a large nesting tree with an eagle's nest in it was deliberately cut down. Why farmers want to destroy eagles is beyond me.

I was interested to hear about magpies eating toad's liver and I would like to relate an incident which entertained us greatly. A few years ago we were invaded by several magpies. They would arrive early in the morning and without a sound they would stand perfectly still, head on one side as if listening. Then all of a sudden down went their beak

into the ground and out would come a witchetty grub. This went on for days. After eating their fill, they would make off to their nests in nearby gum trees to feed their young, which must have been the fattest babies on the peninsular.

Talking of birds: to me, butcher birds are the best songsters in the bush (and suburbs, I might add) and are very knowing. I have in the past fed several by hand and could set the clock by them. They seemed to come from nowhere and swoop on the peewees who had found their supply of mince hidden in banana plants. It was quite amusing to watch.

FROM:
LAURA
Coonamble, NSW

Please listen to my plea to help awaken people to the music of the butcher bird, the harmony of whose notes surpasses, I think, that of the magpie, lovely though that is.

Is it only I who hears the beauty in the drifting pearls from the butcher bird's throat? The magic of this elegance, each bird creating an individual gem, approaches the achievement of the human voice: the notes are performed with care and deliberation and purity of pitch. Whether of short duration or longer, with perhaps an ariatic trill, the song is perfectly modulated, practised, not left to chance. In fancy I call this the Adagio bird, a name befitting the slow cadences.

To me the butcher bird's 'praise to the day', ascending or descending the musical scale, is lyrically expressing a message of consolation or emotional delight; it is an antidote to despondency or a capitulation to joy. Like a song by Kathleen Ferrier, this is a skill crafted with precision that needs no musical accompaniment.

FROM:
ROY LAKE
Maldon
Victoria

I would like to tell you of my experience regarding bird 'courts'. Some months ago I heard a terrific din on our front lawn and walked around to investigate. As I turned the corner of the carport a magpie came out of the sun, nothing on the clock and doing at least Mach.One: a Kamikaze flyer for sure. How he missed me I'll never know. By this time an aerial display was in full swing with magpies taking part in what one could only describe as a 'dogfight'. All this was accompanied by loud warbling and beak snapping. Then, suddenly, they all descended on to the lawn and into two groups. The loud and consistent warbling continued with the birds moving around the lawn, not with any precision or form that I could detect. However, standing to one side were two magpies in a form which I would describe in human terms as 'heads bowed and shoulders hunched'. They stayed this way for some minutes as the warbling then developed into a statement and response situation from the rest of the magpies. When this was over, as if by some prearranged signal they all flew off, some across the road and the rest to the trees around our block.

Maybe it was some form of induction, a 'getting to know you', or some form of magpie freemasonry, as they were all looking very smart in their black and white outfits!

I wonder if anybody would be interested to know that some magpies have a habit of building their nests, using wire, mostly thin copper wire; being soft it would be easier to bend.

FROM:
ROY BISHOP
Rockhampton
Queensland

A couple of years ago I picked up from beneath a tall pine tree one such nest. There would have been at least a hundred feet of wire if all the little pieces were joined end to end. I have shown this nest to my many friends and they were very impressed.

It is absolutely amazing how the birds coiled the wire around and around to form the nest. One thing they forgot to do was to tie the nest to the tree!

Last year I heard a lady describing how she had seen a group of magpies spread-eagled on the ground as though dead. Happily, she went on to relate how a subsequent appearance of a dog caused the magpies to take fright and become airborne, which led to the conclusion that they must have been either sunbaking or sand bathing. Since hearing that program I have been able to photograph a magpie doing exactly as she described. In this case, it being a warm day, he had just enjoyed a shower under the sprinkler on our front lawn and then proceeded to settle himself down in the warm sand on the vacant block next door. Occasionally, he would agitate his wings as though trying to bed himself further into the warm sand. Therefore, I would suggest that he was getting the best of both worlds by sandbathing and sunbaking at the same time.

FROM:
MAURIE JOHANSEN
Eaton, WA

While looking for some poems to include in my resource poem book for 'Kindy' I found this one about magpies. Knowing you like magpies I thought you would like it as well.

Magpies
Magpies sing like violins, or piccolos or flutes.
Perhaps that's why they always fly around in dinner suits.
They dress up like musicians, in white tie, shirt and tails
And give their own renditions of serenades and scales.

FROM:
RAE
COLAHAN
Robina
Queensland

PS. Have discovered other poems about wombats, emus and rosellas.

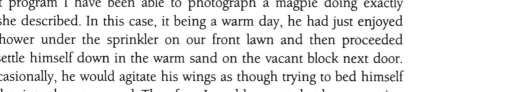

FROM:
BILL CHAPMAN
Tenterfield, NSW

I was prompted to write to you by a flock of galahs. I was watching a flock feeding on a hedge of berry trees and was struck by the parallel between this flock and the flock in Canberra.

It seems that, like galahs, pollies make a lot of noise and do very little. They flock together and each member protects the other from outside dangers, even though they attack each other regularly. They waste more of the available supply than they use and never go anywhere without their mates. Their acrobatic ability when perching and their ability to change direction in mid-flight is well known. Their indignant crest raising and posturing when admonished is legendary. Even when supposedly tamed they have a propensity to bite the hand that feeds them. Maybe the pollies learned all this by parroting the galahs.

Perhaps all politicians, when elected, should be issued with a grey suit and a pink shirt, which would complete the comparison.

The big difference, of course, is that galahs are content to have a full crop and a dead tree for a roost, whereas a pollie demands an exorbitant salary, a mansion, and a massive super payout when he retires. As it is often open season on galahs by the people whose crops they destroy, perhaps the same sort of open season on pollies would also be a good idea.

I am enclosing a little poem on the same subject.

An Australian Prayer
(Dedicated to those conscientious galahs who inhabit that
multi-million dollar aviary in Canberra)

I wish I was a pollie, with a social climbing wife,
I'd live just like a millionaire and have an easy life,
I'd never draw my salary, but use expense accounts,
And never have to show just where I spent these large amounts.
I'd travel in a first class jet wherever I've a mind
With all my staff and family, I can't leave them behind,
And just before elections, the promises I'd make,
I'd give the voters this and that, provided there's a take.
But when the voting's over, the election has been won,
I'd find a dozen reasons why those things cannot be done,
If the workers want a wage increase, a horrifying thought,
I'd put it off until next year, then ballots can be bought.
A wage increase for me and mates is always very dear
To me and mine in Parliament. Let's make it start last year.
To keep the mass subservient, a brand new tax I'd find,
A tax each time you have a pee? I'll keep that one in mind.

If someone calls me crooked, I'd really have to sue,
Or settle it in dollars paid, four hundred thou. will do.
I'd talk and never work, I've staff to do that chore,
It's my belief that working is a proper bloody bore,
I'd have a good assistant who can tell the public where
To contact his assistant, if they really have a care,
Then he in turn can pass them on much further down the line,
They still will get no answers. To a Pollie this is fine.
If they catch me racketeering, I'll simply pass the buck,
And blame the opposition, for raking up the muck.
When I retire my salary would carry on for years,
A million dollars super would not pay for all the tears,
Or all the stress exerted in polishing a chair,
Or all the strain on vocal chords. Oh! life is so unfair,
There's no one who could take my place or occupy my seat,
Or speak the way I've spoken or emulate my feat,
Of putting down all others, who dare to criticise
My running of the country, or my mother's apple pies,
Before I die they'll honour me, a knighthood would be good,
But failing that a portrait or a statue carved in wood,
And when I reach the pearly gates St. Peter he will say,
'A bloody politician!' but he'll have to let me stay.

INTERVIEW: ENID BROWN

At the 'Back to Neilrex' weekend:

'I used to be Enid Galman and my parents came to Neilrex in 1921 when I was only four years old. We had a pretty hard time living here: we had to trap rabbits, pick up dead wood, and for Sunday afternoon sport my sister and I used to kill goannas with our dog. We were cruel little wretches.'

What did you kill the goannas for—to eat them?

'Just for fun—I don't know, everybody killed everything in those days! I don't know why our parents didn't tell us not to kill them.'

Well, I suppose because everything was so abundant in those days. It was like Henry Lawson said, 'it was in the days when the world was wide', and we thought everything was bountiful and there were more goannas up the next tree. But it's not the case today. Have you enjoyed coming back to Neilrex? Did you go to the dance last night?

'Yes, I had a great time at the dance. I haven't danced in this hall for years.'

It's a great little hall, isn't it? Neilrex ought to be proud of this place.

'Yes, we had dances here in this hall when I was a kid. All the mothers and fathers would be dancing and us kids would be down in the corner on rugs and pillows, asleep. These girls here, they're the Montgomerys. They were our next door neighbours and they had seventeen kids.'

Seventeen kids!! Holey Moley!!!

'And we only had two. We spent all out school holidays catching . . .'

Kids?

'Crayfish in their dam. They used to call them cribbens.'

I'm often asked, 'How many people listen to *Australia All Over*, and who are they?'

Well, the answer to the first question is well over a million, and to the second, from the very young to the very old. I don't play 'Twisted Sister' on *Australia All Over* so we probably don't get a lot of teenagers, but we get a lot of youngsters of primary school age.

I've had photographs of babies in cribs with little radios on their pillows—there's one in the book—but that's probably the exception rather than the rule! The kids write letters, often whole classes like 2E of St Joseph's at Port Macquarie, and the Launceston Infants School. They write about why they live where they live. And of course they ring up from various isolated places, and from the cities, too.

They like songs like 'G'day, G'day' and 'Gumboots' and when we do concerts lots of youngsters turn up with their parents and really enjoy themselves.

Julia and a bilby

Just a note to show you what happens when you say, 'The number is double three, nine, two, triple seven.'

FROM:
L. J. SMITH
Corindi Beach
NSW

A Child's Point of View

A little girl, with phone in hand,
And a big frown on her face,
Said, 'Nanna, I can't make my call,
There's no TRIPLE any place.
It's no trouble finding three, three, nine,
The two, or even seven,
But TRIPLE isn't on the dial,
Do you think its gone to Heaven?'
I just might write to Macca,
And say 'How can I ring
When TRIPLE isn't on the dial,
Can you do anything?
I'd really like to talk to you,
'Cos your program is so great,
Till they put that TRIPLE on the dial
I'll just sit here and wait.'

Buckley's Hope is all about a man called Buckley. He was a tall man. He was in the war but he didn't do as he was told. Then he was a convict. Then he ran away. His friend went back to Port Phillip. He met a tribe of Aborigines.

FROM: MARIE ANSELL (9)
Allenstown State
School
Rockhampton, Queensland

I am in grade four. I am nine years of age. I am in Mrs Cox's class. Mrs Cox told us to do research on Buckley's Hope. This is some of the story of Buckley's Hope. There once was a man called William Buckley. William Buckley was born in England in 1780. When he was twenty years old he became a soldier in His Majesty's Army and for a while he was a very good one.

FROM:
MELLISSA BUTTERFIELD
Allenstown State School

I hope you can put the class on *Australia All Over*. There are 30 children in our class. I'm eight years old. My birthday is the 27th of December. I do not listen to it. Mrs Cox said that Chrere and Steven listens to it. Mrs Cox read the story about Buckley's Hope. It is a very good story. I hope you can read about Buckley's Hope.

FROM: ALLANA
Allenstown State School

FROM:
PENNY SCHATKOWSKI
Allenstown State School

Today we read a story about Buckley's Hope. Do you remember the lady that called in and said that William Buckley was an Aborigine? But the book said that William Buckley is a white man. He stayed with the Aborigines for thirty-two years and then went to live with his people. Mrs Cox, and some of 4A, and I, like it very much.

FROM:
2F (TIM & SEAN)
Allenstown State School

The new 2F have written this poem for you. We want you to read it out on the radio. We hope you like it. It's all about Clean Up Australia Day. Because it's the 1st March 1992. We want our country clean so people come to it. And so we don't die. And so pollution doesn't go into the rivers. And so God doesn't feel sad.

FROM:
LACHLAN &
LOUISE
HEATHER
Blaxland
NSW

My sister Louise (8) and I, Lachlan (10) love listening to your program and especially like *Over the Top With Jim*.

I am reading the book and find it very funny. Every Sunday we race to the kitchen to listen to your show. We also like the songs.

FROM:
KIRSTY MAYS
Lakes Entrance
Victoria

My name is Kirsty and I'm a 15-year-old student at Bairnsdale High School. Each morning as I wake from a deep slumber, I automatically reach out to turn on the radio. After much hand searching I open my eyes to find my radio stolen.

Oh no, it's Sunday, and I say 'stolen' because Dad (Barry) has sneaked in very early and 'borrowed' my radio.

No local commercial station (or decent music) for this family on Sunday mornings. By order of the 'head honcho' (Dad) all radios are set to hear 'Macca'.

The minute he hears a rustle in the kitchen a voice from the bowels of the main bedroom orders tea and toast. Fortunately some Sundays he's working so normality reigns.

The crayfishing season in Tasmania is over so the *Mollyanda* is back home for the winter. I believe you saw her in the dock in Hobart. It's great to have Dad home again and we must make the most of the next few months because November comes around very quickly and they'll be off again.

It seems that your show puts Dad in a good mood, ensuring a great day as we head off to the junior football. So I guess it's not so bad after all, though I wouldn't tell Dad!

I'm 10 years old and listen nearly every morning. I have volume one and two and I know every word. *Australia All Over* is my favourite tape. When my cousins Leah and Ozzi visit we do concerts to 'That Song Again', 'G'day, G'day' and all the rest.

THE SAD KOALA

Once upon a time there lived a smart but sad koala. He was always going to the wrong trees. They were not eucalyptus trees, they made him very sick. Luckily someone was walking through the forest (a girl) and she saw him lying on the ground and she started to cry because she loved koalas. She picked him up and took him to her house. Her father was a vet so he looked after the koala and fixed him all up and they all lived happily every after.

This is my story for Save the Koalas Week.

Dear Macca my name is Leah Rath. I live in Marlborough. On Thursday I was climbing a tree with my friend Leah Goodrich. The branch broke and I fell and broke my arm. Lots of people have signed my plaster. I am seven years old.

Greetings from the children in 2F at St. Joseph's Primary, Port Macquarie. At present we are doing a Social Studies unit on Australia, and we have been encouraged to listen to your program to learn more about our great country!

We have written a Mother's Day poem for our wonderful mothers, which we would love to share with all mums in Australia.

What a Wonderful Mother

My Mum, is a great cook,
She also reads me a book.
As she tucks me into bed,
She puts my Ted beside my head
What a wonderful Mother.

Mum often takes me to the park,
Where we play till it gets dark.
My Mum is cheery and bright,
She's never wrong and always right.
What a wonderful Mother.

Mum is smiling and pretty,
She's intelligent, smart and witty.
My Mum is loving, kind and beautiful,
She's always funny, sharing and helpful.
What a wonderful Mother.

Mum is extra super-duper,
She is never a party pooper.
Mum really likes to sleep in,
But she wakes up to the sound of the wind
What a wonderful Mother.

Mum is generous and always there,
Because she really, really cares.
My Mum is well dressed,
Mum you're the best.
What a wonderful Mother.

FROM:
ROWENA WILTSHIRE
Coleambally
NSW

G'day! This is Rowena, in Coleambally. Coleambally's in the Riverina, near Griffith. This morning I heard you play a beaut little song called Down in the Riverina. I was soon singing along and I thought I'd drop you a line.

Coleambally's a small country town of about 600, (not including the farming district), and quite modern, twenty-three years old.

We live on a farm ten kilometres out of town. We have sheep and grow wheat and rice. We also have chooks, cats, poddy lambs, a young kangaroo and three horses, which my two sisters and I ride. The joey was found in its dead mother's pouch after a collision with a car and was brought to us to look after. It is very young, very thin and bony and hairless. At this stage it shouldn't even be out of the pouch but we are doing all we can to keep it alive.

Huge numbers of our native animals are being killed on the roads, as a result of careless driving or because the animals are being blinded by the headlights, and in the confusion the car hits them. But how many people actually stop and check to see if the animal's injured or has a baby? It's our responsibility to preserve our native environment and native animals. And it's not just kangaroos; wombats, possums and many others are dying needlessly, and often through no fault of their own.

Now that I've said my piece, congratulations on a fantastic Australian show. I look forward to getting up and switching on the radio, having brekkie and enjoying the Aussie music and stories.

SHOPPING TROLLEYS

The Shopping Trolley Saga started on *Australia All Over* in about 1987 when I mentioned that I'd seen a clipping in a newspaper about a supermarket that was charging a $10 deposit for shopping trolleys. Apparently people had been taking the trolleys and trashing them to use the bottoms for barbeque grills and—as one of our correspondents, Alan Ellem from Perth, said—taking the wheels to swap meets.

After I mentioned shopping trolleys on the program I had a letter from John Bourne of Biloela. He's a dentist by trade but a comedian and a cynic by nature. His letter is included in this chapter.

And then I received hundred of letters about shopping trolleys, plus photographs. These are also a testimony to Australians' sense of humour.

'The Trolley', seen at the Human Factor Exhibition
at Caneland Shoppingtown, Mackay, Queensland

SHOPPING TROLLEYS

(John started the ball rolling with this letter!)

FROM:
JOHN BOURNE
Biloela
Queensland

A couple of weeks ago I was patching a tank. It was one of a group on a ridge above the house surrounded by vine scrub. There were some unusual noises coming from the scrub but I didn't pay much attention at the time, assuming it was probably wallabies or scrub turkeys doing one of their things; anyway, was much more concerned with the tarry muck I was working with, trying to get it into the cracks in the tank and keeping it out of eyes, ears, hair and so forth.

It was only when listening to some of the phone-ins that a couple of pennies dropped and the strange metallic rattling sounds seemed to make sense, so I snuck up the ridge behind the house and into the scrub.

Sure enough, there they were. I only had a fleeting glimpse, as, with a rattle of wheels, they disappeared deeper into the scrub, but enough to identify a nesting pair of supermarket trolleys—the flashing chrome of the slender female in strong contrast to the chipped orange paint of the heavier, more thickset male.

In front of me was their nest—a mound of leaves and debris, similar to a scrub turkey and, protruding from the top, the shiny grey edge of a brand new PCD (Port Curtis Dairy) milk crate. So, part of the puzzle seems to have fallen into place—milk crates are a larval form of shopping trolleys, it would seem. Therefore, the shopping trolleys that we find in all sorts of unlikely places are either mature adults in the process of migrating from their supermarket hosts into the bush, to mate, nest and produce juvenile milk crates, or in some cases they may be young shopping trolleys, searching for a supermarket where they can mature.

There are obviously still a lot of unknowns: for example, where does the metamorphosis take place? Is the habit of milk crates of collecting in groups under the mattresses of Sydney flat dwellers part of this process? Do they require intermediate hosts other than milkmen?

I suspect that there is possibly an aquatic phase in the cycle as well. Some years ago, during our own aquatic phase, we frequently sighted milk crates sunning themselves on the mud flats as we motored into a secluded inlet. Upon anchoring, and going back in the dinghy to pick them up, they would invariably be gone, with no tracks to indicate whether they had slipped into the water, retreated into the mangroves, or merely burrowed deeper into the mud. This aquatic phase may explain the presence of dead shopping trolleys at the bottom of Tineroo Dam— perhaps in their larval stage these trolleys had spent their aquatic phase in the dam, and, in maturity, had experienced an uncontrollable urge to return to this environment—something akin to the force which drives spawning salmon to return to the stream of their birth.

There is, as I said before, much still not known in this field. It will require many hours of observation and study by dedicated individuals.

This type of research is time consuming and expensive. Perhaps we should be seeking Government assistance. I would be prepared to accept a Commonwealth grant to enable me to study full time the behaviour of milk crates when washed up on secluded beaches. I suspect there may be some connection between this and the dextro-rotation of marooned thongs. (This is the phenomenon where, if you find a left thong washed up on a beach, all the other thongs encountered for the next two miles will be left. When in disgust you throw the left thong away, all further thongs encountered will be right.)

There is still so much that we don't know about nature and its laws in this great country of ours—the opportunities are boundless.

FROM:
MURIEL COURTENAY
Bundaberg
Queensland

Do those shopping trolleys en route to New Zealand realise what is in store for them? In Auckland they will have their name changed to 'trundlers' and will be housed in trundler parks not trolley bays.

Should any be diverted to New Caledonia by wind and sea, these trolleys will become 'chariots' in the supermarkets.

Meanwhile spare a thought for the thousands of our Aussie battler trolleys shivering in draughty car parks across the nation, the wind whistling through their metal ribs. Maybe we could get Jenny Kee to design them sweaters for the winter.

FROM: PHILLIP LONG
Toowoomba
Queensland

I have followed with interest the shopping trolley saga. Now that national attention has been drawn to the plight of various shopping trolleys I feel I must answer a 'calling' which I have felt deep within me for some time.

I feel heartbroken about the lack of good quality young shopping trolleys in our town of Toowoomba. Not only have most of our trolleys got birth defects such as wobbly wheels, we haven't got enough trolleys.

My research shows there is a chronic fertility problem in shopping trolleys in Toowoomba. I have been in touch with other researchers and we agree that this infertility problem could spread across the world.

We have formed a group in Toowoomba to open an in vitro fertilisation clinic for shopping trolleys. At first only local shopping trolleys will be serviced, but we will eventually be offering our in vitro fertilisation procedures to many countries around the world. This new export business will no doubt help Australia's balance of trade and we will shortly be approaching the federal government for a subsidy.

Any listener who wishes to make a tax deductible donation to this worthwhile cause can donate at any store using shopping trolleys.

FROM:
ADRIAN PAUL
Coffs Harbour, NSW

I heard the rather far-fetched story from the owner of the *Bounty* about the armada of shopping trolleys defecting from Australia and sailing to New Zealand. Being a natural sceptic I decided to make some investigations for myself and so, taking the advantage of a beautiful Coffs Harbour Sunday morning, my family and I went aboard the *Bounty* and were given a fascinating talk about the ship.

During his talk the owner mentioned the shopping trolley armada and happened to let slip that there were two trolleys below deck, but they were too shy to come on deck and talk to strangers. He added that below deck was off limits to all, bar crew and passengers, so this made me even more suspicious about his armada story.

Risking both life and limb, while my children distracted his attention, I managed to sneak below. There I found the horrifying scene of one shopping trolley in complete agony, having had all its wheels removed to prevent escape. A second trolley (a female) was in a complete swoon, having been chained to the bunk which Mel Gibson slept on during the 1980s remake of the movie.

In a hurried conversation with the first trolley I learnt the real truth. True to the real Captain Bligh image, whilst moored in Sydney the Captain had press-ganged (or should I say 'checkout-chicked') a large number of shopping trolleys into service, with the plan of using them as giant lobster pots and establishing a whole new industry in the Pacific Islands.

Fortunately, in the midst of a Force 10 gale whilst off Port Macquarie, most of these trolleys managed to jump ship, formed an armada and were last seen heading in the direction of Pitcairn Island, where they plan to set up a new trolley colony, in true Bounty mutineer tradition. With the trolleys coming from a number of different genetically-branded sources there is little chance of the risk of in-breeding, which can of course occur in such relatively small and isolated colonies.

So there you have it, Macca—the ghost of Captain Bligh lives again, riding the high South Seas and striking fear into the heart of every freedom-loving shopping trolley in the Pacific region.

Let's hope they make it—after all, anything would be preferable to either life-long service in a supermarket or to serving the rest of one's days as a lobster pot!

SHOPPING TROLLEYS

FROM:
GIL WAHLQUIST
Mudgee, NSW

While on a visit to England recently I was swan-upping on the Kennett River at Reading when I saw the swans circling an object in the water. I was seated outside the 'Jolly Angler' hotel at the time and it was no trouble for me to lean forward and spy the object of their attention— a shopping trolley.

The presence of the trolley in the river is a mystery. The Kennett River runs into the Thames River. Was the trolley making its way upstream to the place of its birth, or was it headed in the other direction, down the Thames, on yet another re-enactment voyage to Australia for the bicentennial?

After pondering these points over a warm beer or two I pulled out the Pentax and took some documentary evidence. You can't keep a good shopping trolley down!

Oh, in case you're wondering about swan-upping, it is the exclusive right of vintners, wine merchants, that is, to conduct swan-upping on the Thames. Swan-upping is the counting of the number of swans on the river.

FROM:
JUDI COX
Kenmore
Queensland

I heard some mention of shopping trolleys and realized how secretive they have been lately. I think I have an answer, though I fear it is a sinister one.

In many neighbourhoods at the moment there is much new growth. Nestled among the native trees have suddenly appeared McDonald biggamacca, Kentuckii nonflavum, and Sizzlerphyllum quickum, to name just a few.

Well, the neat gardens surrounding these new growths are attracting unusual visitors.

Shopping trolleys, obviously sick and tired of carting slow foods such as snail bait and frozen chips, are drawn to fast food outlets. There they lurk, hiding under bushes, sniffing the smells, their emaciated frames aquiver with delight. Occasionally, driven by hunger, they take a bite out of an unsuspecting patron or a parked car.

But wait, I hear you say, could there be a hidden agenda here? Could they be doing a 'feastability' study?

Will we be seeing a chain of MacTrolleys across the nation (One Nation, of course), with the shopping trolley proudly displayed on the roof, or will the wheels fall off the whole idea?

I'm sure your listeners will report in at the first sign of a MacTrolley-led recovery.

SHOPPING TROLLEYS

FROM:
WALLIE WILSON
Gladstone
Queensland

I have been following the saga of the shopping trolley over the months and I must tell you about the migratory habits of the shopping trolleys from Gladstone in Central Queensland.

Recently at a shopping centre I saw hundreds of superseded trolleys being discreetly loaded onto a semi-trailer in the early morning. They had been made redundant and were replaced by shiny new trolleys with red plastic wheels that roll easily and will go in the direction that you steer them.

My first impression was that these trolleys, in their latter years, were migrating north to Cairns for the winter. But there was something wrong! Some of the trolleys were resisting being loaded onto the truck. Trolleys were locking up their wheels and bearings were squealing in defiance of their handlers. Some wheels were even shaking violently with the fear of their uncertain fate. It was then that I realised that this was mass trolley genocide. I was horrified: this was no way to end the life of faithful servants who had served the shoppers of Gladstone for years. I had visions of files of trolleys being driven against their will into a mega metal muncher and being reduced to scrap metal. Surely there must be a more fitting fate for aged trolleys. They could be placed in the care of a kind family and see their retired years out as a toy trolley and quietly play with the children. Alternatively, they could hold indoor plants and sit quietly in the corner of a rumpus room enjoying the company of the family pets.

I felt a twinge of sadness to see these old faithful servants being pensioned off in this undignified manner. I paused and reflected on all the years of service that these trolleys had given Gladstone. I have fond memories of trolley number 33, to which I was particularly attached. I would seek out number 33 in the line of trolleys when I went to the supermarket. Old 33 carried my groceries and children around the shopping aisles, rarely protesting or trying to pull in the opposite direction. I felt quite emotional to think that somewhere in amongst those dented, rusty trolleys on that truck was old 33. I would never see him again.

Lest we forget.

I am writing to make an appeal to your listeners to support the Disabled Shopping Trolleys Fund. Which of us gives a second thought to the trolley we push around with a dislocated or arthritic wheel, except to curse at its slowness? Do we ever try to alleviate the suffering of a shopping trolley with rust dermo? Do we ever consider that many of the poor trolleys' ailments are due to trolley abuse? I appeal to all listeners to give our less fortunate shopping trolleys a fair go. They should not be overloaded or left out in the rain. Neither should they be subjected to

FROM:
RICHARD
GROSS
Saratoga
NSW

wheelies around the supermarket aisles. I feel that if we do not treat our shopping trolleys right they will organise (together with the Wire Coat Hangers Union) and there'll be a Chrome Ban on supermarkets and we'll all have to carry our own groceries; or, worse still, they'll picket the car parks. I have already seen small groups of shopping trolleys attempting this, and if you keep your eyes open you'll see what I mean.

FROM:
FRED WARD
Bairnsdale
Victoria

My Landcruiser was assaulted recently by an in-season shopping trolley in a busy Bairnsdale street.

Parked by the kerb in this street, my hard-top 4X4 attracted the attention of a Hereford shopping trolley which had been joined by another of the same breed on the footpath. By coming up on my blind side from the path with apparent amorous intent, the trolleys were unnoticed until I went to drive off. As soon as I engaged the clutch there arose a nasty dragging sound and I switched off and went around to investigate. There to my great surprise was this red and white couple mounting the vehicle step! Trying not to attract too much attention I retrieved the pair from this embarrassing position, herded them up onto the sidewalk again and left them still joined together.

Climbing back into the Cruiser I restarted and let out the clutch pedal— 'rattle rattle—rasp rasp' from the left side and when I again dismounted there they were—at it again!!!

Feeling pretty exposed to the gaze of the gathering crowd, I looked about for some sort of secure place to yard the trolleys. Nearby there was a rubbish bin firmly anchored to the concrete. I tethered the beasts to it and quickly drove off. Later, when I drove past the spot again, I was not surprised to see that the two had been joined by another of the same breed—another case of the eternal triangle, eh?

The local shopping trolleys seem to be a highly neurotic lot. When looking into the clear depths of the Mitchell River for bream one day, I spotted a trolley that had obviously commited suicide by diving into those chilly depths.

I heard you are interested in shopping trolleys, so I thought I would drop a line. I, too, love the beasts. Do you breed them or race them?

I'm on the breaking-in side myself. I take on the job of breaking in the new trolleys as the need arises. They are very flighty but hard-working beasts, so the casualty rate is pretty high and I get a lot of work breaking in the replacements.

Then there are trolleys for the new supermarkets; that's a mass

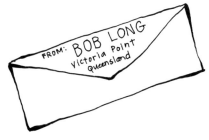

FROM: BOB LONG
Victoria Point
Queensland

production job. I've had to break in several hundred at times. Plenty of work, good money.

With an offsider, I usually put up a breaking yard in the back corner of the shop among the vegies, and handle and ride them in there for the first time. It's a great thrill to have a great crowd of shoppers cheering and shouting when I ride a bad one. After the breaking yard I have to ride them around the shop until they're quiet enough to handle the crowds without kicking over the jam, etc.

I had one very bad one recently. He threw his legs every way but straight. I thought I had him steadied down by the time I got to the check-outs. One was blocked with the usual chain and, quick as a flash, my steed swerved and went under the chain. Being good, I anticipated, and as he went under, I went over. I was quicker than him and I landed in front of him. He nudged me so I hooked my arms over his front and stuck my legs straight out. So there I was slithering along on the rowels of my big Mexican-type spurs.

Of course, he bolted. The doors opened and in no time I'm out in the car park among the BMWs and Volvos. My spurs, being imported, had no roller bearings in the rowels, so in no time they're red hot and I'm leaping from spur to spur to keep from getting burnt. Things were pretty desperate. Luckily, as we went by the rear door of a Volvo station wagon it opened and, quick as light, a lovely young woman reached down and plucked me off the front of that raging trolley and threw champagne over my red hot spurs. I can recall her murmuring 'You are so brave' as she soothed me. Some time later, when she put me back down in the car park, the trolley had disappeared.

I'd appreciate it if you would spread the word. If anyone sights an outlaw trolley with a breaking-in saddle, crupper and breast-plate on, let me know. The finder can have the bridle, I've got a spare, but I need the other gear. I've still got 278 trolleys to break in!

I'll bet you've been wondering what has happened to me since I finished breaking in the shopping trolleys in the supermarket.

The truth is, I've been droving the beasts. I got the chance to go out west of the Darling Downs to the Big W station, and pick up 500 stud bull trolleys for delivery to Toowoomba. I jumped at the chance, for the money was good.

I put together a good droving plant and hired two beautiful young girls to help. They were to help with the herd but had mainly to be able to play bridge at night around the camp. I think you'll agree it's a poor droving plant without a bridge four at night.

ALSO FROM:
BOB LONG
Victoria Point
Queensland

I also got a very old fella to tail the riding trolleys and shift camp. He could play bridge too.

Well, we counted out of the Big W yards 500 of the best stud bull trolleys. They were very well grown, though you could see their ribs, and they had a silvery sheen to them which showed good health. They were pretty wild too. They'd been reared on the best of feed, mainly wire brush and pot scour, so we went along fast for the first few days.

We averaged five rushes a night for the first week, and I couldn't keep them on the camp. Eventually, I drove them over a few sets of up-turned harrows and tenderised their feet a bit and that steadied them down. Until then, I'd had little or no time to play bridge with the girls in the evenings, and the old fellow, out ahead, was spending all his time seeking out wire brushes and similar feed for the night camps. By the time he'd belled and hobbled the riding trolleys, done the camp chores and a trick on the night trolley, he was tuckered out and turned in.

The mob went along fairly well, and except for the odd eating of a motor bike or small car, they soon settled down. They're very noisy beasts though, and it was common to have thousands lining the stock route to see us all swing by.

The big trouble started when we got to Toowoomba. We had to go through in the dead of night, of course, and got to the heart of the city when someone dropped a milk can on the concrete, and the whole mob were clanking, rattling and running. It was the worst trolley rush I've ever seen.

We all had first class trolleys under us, but try as we might we could neither wheel them or steady them and it rapidly got to where the mob scattered. For two days and a night the whole city was in an uproar while we were busily going into all sorts of places to root the trolleys out and muster them back into a mob. In the suburbs those bull trolleys got into the laundries and back yards where every house had a laundry trolley and they're all females. I couldn't help but notice how reluctant the laundry trolleys were to retreat behind the closed laundry doors!

Well, eventually, we got the shopping trolleys mustered and only a few were lost. I'll bet, if you look around Toowoomba you'll see the odd bull trolley, lost and forlorn. I was docked for the few I lost. Still, I couldn't help but notice, as we moved the mob through the town to the delivery yards, the large number of pretty laundry trolleys standing in the driveways, hip-shot, cud-chewing, eyelashes on cheeks, and a self satisfied look on the face. It will, indeed, be interesting to see what eventuates in the town in a few months' time. The bull trolleys looked happy too.

SHOPPING TROLLEYS

Shopping trolleys are upsetting the Logan City Council, which has decided to impound wayward members of the species and charge supermarkets to have them released. Shopping trolleys have been blamed for inciting dogs to bark, the disappearance of pet cats, the increase in house burglaries, pregnancy and the waylaying of husbands on their way home from work. Some learned, local public bar scientists believe their activities in local parks have a direct effect on the ozone layer.

Well, Council has decided enough is enough. One of our more intellectual Aldermen (if such an animal exists) suggested that they be 'press ganged' into the Royal Woodridge Navy. This idea was enthusiastically received until it was realised Logan City didn't possess a deep water port (or any port for that matter except in the local bottle shop). A Royal Woodridge Air Force was ruled out for similar reasons and the thought of a military coup led the Mayor to rule out any thought of a Royal Woodridge Army.

At the time of writing there seems no solution in sight, which worries me, in particular, as I live within walking distance of five supermarkets. Logan City Council has written to other Councils in the region and a joint committee may be formed—yes, the panacea for all ailments, a committee. Will keep you informed if there are any exciting new developments.

Down South

Two weeks ago one of your listeners floored me. Fortunately, I was still in bed, so the injuries were minimal. The surprising event was when the gentleman rang from Davis Base on the Antarctic mainland. The wonders of modern telecommunications still amaze me.

Although I have not wintered down south, I have spent the last year on a photographic project at Adelaide University working with the Mawson Institute for Antarctic Research. Every day I am surrounded by the work of the photographer Frank Hurley and the many artifacts from the Antarctic expeditions led by Sir Douglas Mawson.

During the course of my project I am constantly surprised by the number of people who express an interest in the Antarctic, or who know someone who has been down south.

Unfortunately, my first voyage south on the *Nella Dan* ended in news headlines as those back home shared the events leading up to the scuttling of the *Nella Dan* off Macquarie Island last December. I am hoping to get to the continent this summer so I will be able to complete my project.

·IMPROVE·YOUR·RADIO·RECEPTION·

If you're out in the bush on a Sunday morning, and you can't get 'Australia All Over' on your transistor radio, here are a couple of solutions.

I. Find a wire fence and hold the transistor radio on it. Rotate for the best reception.

OR

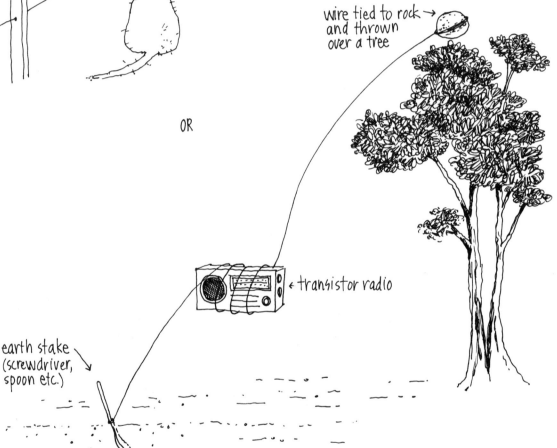

wire tied to rock → and thrown over a tree

← transistor radio

earth stake (screwdriver, spoon etc.)

2. Throw a rock tied with wire over a tree.
Wrap the wire around your transistor radio, and use a spoon or screwdriver as an earth stake.
✳ STAY WELL AWAY FROM ANY POWER LINES

From Bob Nicol - (retired CSIRO electronic technician) *Barakee, Armidale, NSW*

ENVIRONMENT

As I think I said somewhere else, the thing that makes Australia different, and therefore makes us different (apart from our Aboriginal heritage), is our environment, because it impinges on everything we do.

A big change has come over Australia in the last decade because most of us realise what damage has been done to Australia in just two hundred years. But I'm not going to tell you what a disgraceful mess the Murray, Hawkesbury, Shoalhaven or Derwent Rivers are in, or how governments in Australia, state and federal, really don't care about the environment but pretend they do.

Fixing up the mess is really up to you, because *you're* the government—or at least that's my concept of democracy. Once *you* start to care, watch it change.

Grass Tree (*Xanthorrhea*)

*Ian and Brian Cooke at the South Australian
Landcare Awards ceremony in December 1990*

Our Wattle

Down along the rivers' banks
And on the distant hills
Like God had dropped a can of paint
The golden wattle spills.

When winter blows her icy blasts
Complete with hail and snow
The golden wattle bursts its buds
And sets the land aglow.

The pride of all Australian hearts
Acclaimed by pen and voice
The emblem of our native land
Could be no better choice.

And throughout all the length and breadth
Of this great land of ours
Some family member holds the torch
Of this our Queen of flowers.

And if I move to foreign climes
No matter where I go
Though years pass I will not forget
Our golden wattle's glow.

FROM:
WILBUR OLSEN
Poowong East
Victoria

FROM:
LESLEY MILLS
Blackwood
South Australia

Until I discovered you, there was never any reason to lie in bed on a Sunday morning! But now my husband and self are unable to get up until we have had a cuppa and listened to your entertaining show— meeting and learning about this wondrous land and its colourful people. I often hear you discussing concerns about our environment and this is why I am writing—in the hope that you will spread my message.

I am a mature age student (never too late to learn!) and have spent this semester learning about the environment and how our lifestyle is affecting the ecological system. The Middle East crisis and the increase in the price of petrol have made me think about life without oil—no winter heating, no fuel for the car, a shut down of many industries etc. I wonder how many people realise that oil forms under special conditions and takes millions of years to do so. It is not an everlasting resource and yet we use all natural resources as if they were. Throughout the history of mankind at no other stage has the human race been so wasteful—we have become the 'throw-away' society. In order to maintain our lifestyle we are depleting the very natural resources that the environment has unselfishly given. In return we are changing the ecological balance so vital for the wellbeing of this planet. So I urge every Australian to think about ways in which they can conserve our natural resources and ensure the maintenance of this wondrous planet. Simple, small changes such as using a string bag to carry groceries, or growing a few vegetables to reduce processing and packaging, will ultimately have a positive effect on the environment. We, the people of Australia, all have the power to enhance and preserve the environment, making sure the environment meets the needs of future generations.

Have just been enjoying a late breakfast with your program when you read a letter from an artist, a lover of the bush, who expressed his concern about the burning of the bushland.

He implies that cattlemen cannot co-exist with the natural inhabitants of the bush.

I would like to reply to this rather common, ill-informed view of burning off.

Since time began, bushfires have occurred naturally by lightning. Anyone who lives in the remoter areas of Australia still experiences this. After a good wet season with the prolific growth of grasses, the subsequent dry season, then the build-up to the next wet with its accompanying dry thunderstorms, it is not unusual to see several bushfires start up in one tinder dry afternoon.

The Aboriginals also used fire as a hunting method. We learned this when we lived in the Great Sandy Desert. Fires were lit in the spinifex and went their own way till the wind blew them back on themselves, extinguishing them. Sometimes these fires burned for days uncontrolled in the desert spinifex. The controlled burning, which is carried out with the help of fire breaks, etc, saves untold thousands of acres being devastated by fires.

I would like to put in a word for the reptiles. You see, Australia is a very special place for reptiles, but most Australians don't seem to appreciate that.

FROM:
JO VANDERMARK
O'Connor, ACT

As we know, Australia is the most under-inhabited continent in the world. Approximately eighty per cent of Australia is arid, and where there isn't much water, there isn't much food!

Now, reptiles don't get their energy from food as we mammals do because they are solar-powered. In fact, a reptile needs only one-tenth of the amount of food a mammal requires. So you can see that in a country where food is in short supply, if a reptile can survive on ten per cent of the amount of food a mammal needs, it has a big advantage— and there certainly isn't any shortage of solar power in most of Australia!

Incidentally, we think we're pretty smart because we have just begun to tinker with solar power—the odd solar house, solar-heated swimming pool, solar car—but reptiles have been using solar power for 200 million years! Did you know those funny looking plates running down the centre back of the Stegosaurus were actually solar panels?

We could learn a lot from reptiles.

The subject is about the snake on Sydney Central Station, 1930. Having worked on Central for many years before the war I have seen many changes 'under the clock' such as the old 'P' class engines which used to run to Penrith and Liverpool, the back-up locos for the Epping bank and the clouds of sulphur smoke which used to envelop the whole station. But the big excitement was the carpet snake which used to slither up the ventilation pipe to meet the folk on Central Station.

FROM: BILL ALLPORT
Ryde, NSW

You can imagine the rumpus if this happened at the Sydney Airport today! There were phones ringing, people shouting and general confusion. Eventually Wally was summoned from the refreshment rooms to come and get him, it being Wally's job to look after the snake. So, nicely curled around the man's shoulder, he was transported down the back steps to his den.

Many people do not know how vast the station is. It is a honeycomb of tunnels. There are ice works, boilers, butcher's shop and kitchens. Our friend the snake kindly kept the rats and mice under control.

Heard your discourse on snakes and heartily support your stand. I made it my business to read as much as I could on snakes after a little incident with a snake a few years back on the banks of the Brunswick River.

FROM:
DIANE COOK
North Balgowlah, NSW

A child of the city in those days, I was camping with my two boys, then about eight and ten years old, in the caravan park right on the river.

Walking along the grass by the river, I came across a little green snake heading towards the main camping area. Not knowing much about snakes in those days, I ran for the nearest 'local' I could see. Excitedly, I described the snake to him and asked him to identify it for me. Grabbing a shovel, he said 'Just show it to me, lady' and off we went.

Upon locating the little green snake, I expected the mower man to lift it up with the shovel and hurry it away to a safer spot away from the children in the park. Stupid lady...to my complete shock and horror, he proceeded to chop it into pieces with the shovel! I was absolutely disgusted. We still didn't know whether it was poisonous or not!

I vowed then and there I would find out more about snakes and educate people about them; make them realise snakes will get out of your way if you give them a chance!

My poor little snake turned out to be a harmless green tree snake and I was sick at heart for months to think my ignorance had caused the death of an innocent creature.

On the subject of carpet snakes, I thought you may like to hear the tale of our family.

We visited my husband's mother at Tullibigeal one Easter and found a carpet snake in the bushes. Bill (my husband) put it in the glove box of our car to take back to the farm, it being so good for catching mice and rats, etc.

On arriving back at the farm the snake had disappeared! We looked all through the engine and the car—our son Martin, who had his clarinet with him, even tried 'playing it out'—but to no avail.

We came back to Sydney and took our three boys and a cousin off to see the Easter Show. It was raining when we left. We tried to put the wipers on, but no go. So we went to the local auto electrician to renew the fuse (as we thought). This nice man got under the dash board to renew the fuse, and he came out WHITE! and tells us 'There's a b... snake in there'. Yes, he had crawled through the hole in the glove box and settled along the space for the wipers! Someone produced a bag, we undid the grille over the wipers and up he came.

After all the razzle-dazzle quietened down we took the snake to the local produce store. The store owner said 'The poor thing is hungry, he hasn't eaten anything for days.' He was right, of course; we had travelled the 300 miles home with the snake resting peacefully. Just as well it hadn't rained!

FROM:
VALDA ROSENBERG
East Hills, NSW

Working in wetlands, snakes are a common sight. We often see them—that is, their tails—disappearing behind a tussock here, under a shrub there. They have never been a problem and, yes, seem harmless enough. Here in southern South Australia they are mostly copper heads and tigers.

FROM:
NAOMI
Adelaide
South Australia

However one summer day, high thirty degrees, I was sampling around the edge of Hindmarsh Island in the mouth of the Murray River. We would jump out of the boat and walk through the reeds to the shore. As I approached a thick stand of reeds in about thigh-deep water, there was a crash-crash-crash noise. At first I thought it was a kangaroo or a swan flapping its wings on the water. But from twenty yards off to the right I saw a tiger snake, thrashing its way through the reeds, coming very fast toward me. When it got just opposite me, about two yards off, it dived into the water and shot right at my legs, thrashing about in the water and, yes, trying to bite! Fortunately I had a metre ruler in my hand (to measure depth) and I tried to beat it off. After a while all went quiet, but then it came up behind me and tried to attack from there. Eventually I beat it off and it swam to a patch of reeds that stood between the boat and me! There it swam about with its head up, watching, whilst I wondered how to get back to the boat before another attack.

By the way, I was wearing a wetsuit as protection from snakes, but because it was so bloody hot, had tied the arms and body round my waist. If I had taken a couple more steps, it would have struck me waist high. With only my bathers on, it would've been fatal.

So much for snakes that mind their own business!

We live on the bank of the Murray six miles down stream from Morgan. We get a few snakes around our house, like one wrapped around the leg of the bed when the wife was going to bed one night and another wrapped around the taps in the bath. I've killed four in the house and one in the canary cage after it had knocked off two canaries. One got into the finches' aviary and we lost six birds that time (greedy bugger). But it was too fat to get out through the netting, so Jessie got to him with the long handled shovel. Our best year was thirty-eight snakes. I'll bet Jessie is one of the few women who takes a shot gun with her when she puts out her washing!

FROM:
AUSSIE ATKINSON
Morgan
South Australia

I heard that lady describe how she had been nobbled by a king brown snake while getting water from a dam in the evening and thought her experience quite horrific.

Yesterday was very warm and while outdoors we were watching out

FROM:
JOY
BROUGHTON
Port Lincoln
South Australia

for snakes. That night I dreamt that a brown snake had curled itself around my arm and I could feel its horrid warm breath on my neck. I dared not move a muscle in my body because I knew it would bite me if I did. Its tongue was flicking and fanning my skin; then, as I panicked and thrashed my arms around, I could feel needle-like teeth puncture my flesh. I gave a yelp of pain and leapt out of bed at four in the morning. Half asleep, and in the dark, I tottered down to the kitchen. As my bare feet padded over the cold kitchen tiles I hoped I didn't tread on any sleeping death adders. I poured myself a glass of milk because my throat was terribly dry and as I propped myself up against the refrigerator, I thought, heavens, I hope I never get bitten by a real snake!

So the woman who is recovering from snake bite certainly has my sympathy.

FROM:
S. HARTSHORN
Silkwood
Queensland

A brief note for people who are reliant on rainwater tanks for drinking and who have pet snakes in their house. Please make sure your overflow spout has a flap valve so Mr Joe Blake can escape. A brown tree snake decided to explore the down pipe in my tank and drowned. It decomposed, polluted the water (not his fault) and made me ill for a couple of days, as I always drink two glasses of water pre-dawn.

FROM: LINDA BROWN
Manjimup, Western
Australia

Where we live, dangerous snakes are extremely common and if there are any harmless ones we have yet to hear their names in these parts. We are not snake lovers but neither are we terrified. Our farm is completely surrounded by native forest, the nearest being only sixty yards from the house. Tiger snakes are thick in this area and dugites quite common. The tiger snakes are not very big, usually three to four feet, sometimes larger, and probably live on frogs. Our rainfall in recent years averages 35-43 inches a year and so there are plenty of wet areas for frogs. The dugites are usually larger, up to five or six feet long.

No-one hereabouts thinks it's unusual to have healthy cows drop dead from snakebite in summer months, and you would be hard pressed to find a farmer who hasn't lost cows.

If we see a snake in the bush we leave him alone. If he is near the house we kill him. We once had a tiger snake spend the winter under the kitchen floor. Another hibernated under a piece of tin left under the mulberry tree.

I do agree that snakes normally try to escape. They do not make an unprovoked attack. But the snake's idea of escape is under the house or in the shed! One hid under the lawnmower. Would you like to bend down to switch on the fuel tap next to his beady eye? So what are we to do? What about children and dogs? I have personally killed six snakes with a spade and my husband said that was too dangerous and bought a 12-gauge shotgun.

A small point of interest is that almost every time I've discovered a snake near the house I've been alerted by the birds. We have three or four families of gorgeous wrens living permanently in our garden. We have no cats. They make loud insistent warning calls at the first sign of a snake and do not stop until it is out of range or dead.

 # INTERVIEW: SHEILA McKELLAR

At Rockhampton Railway Station:

McKellar's a very famous name, isn't it?

'Well, my married name is Nathan, but they all know me as Sheila McKellar.'

And you're related to...?

'Dorothea.'

What sort of a lady was Dorothea?

'Glorious! I met her when I was six, at her home. Lady McKellar and Dorothea lived at a place called 'Rosemont' in Edgecliff. I remember Lady McKellar had a beautiful green Rolls Royce and a chauffeur called Banner who was always dressed in a beautiful green suit to match. The McKellars always had Rolls Royces: they were a very wealthy family. Dorothea had a chauffeur called Duffy, and she looked after him until the day he died. She just adored Duffy, and Duffy adored her, too.'

Did she ever recite any of her poems for you?

'No, she was very quiet, very reserved. Her mother was deaf but she used to lip-read Dorothea very well. I have a photograph of Eric, Dorothea's brother. Eric was a wonderful polo player and I have a photograph of his six horses. They're beautiful.'

Can I ask how old you are, Sheila?

'Seventy-three.'

And you've lived in Rocky all your life? What sort of a place is it?

'Oh, wonderful! I couldn't run my own home down, could I?'

WELL, I LOVE IT!

'Well, I love it!' These words by Jessie Dunstone
gladdened hearts all over the country. Jessie
came from Swan Hill in Victoria and worked
at the Swan Hill Pioneer Settlement where,
among other things, she made damper for the
tourists. After a lifetime of service to the
community, she was declared 'a living treasure'
by the Victorian Tourist Commission. Ian met
her when she was being toured around and that's
how those famous words came into being.

Never 'eard of it

It was Dave from down Snake Gully
That won a trip for two
In a guessing game in the General Store
At Tangmalangmaloo.

So he and Mabel went abroad
And bussed all Europe round
They gaped at all the famous sights
And trod the hallowed ground.

But London Mabel toured alone
For Dave had had his fill
He took a stool in a Watney's bar
Between the taps and till.

And there in peace and the cool half-light
Dave sat and sighed and drank
Till he stuck up conversation
With a fellow-tourist Yank.

They talked about the weather
And they bought each other beer
They grew more chummy glass by glass
With alcoholic cheer.

'Tell me where you hail from friend'
Said the Yank with a tipsy sway
'I'm over from Australia, mate,
From out Snake Gully way'.

'Well I've toured England for a year'
the Yank said with a frown,
'And Ireland, too, I saw it all
From Cork to County Down.'

'I thought I knew the UK well'
And he poured another beer
'But I never heard of Australia,
Is it very far from here?'

Dave nearly dropped his beer in shock
He surely dropped his jaw
And he then dropped all mateship
And civility for sure.

'You've never heard of Aussie?
Good God, I'm at a loss
It's that bloody great big island
Beneath the Southern Cross.'

'Does three million square miles of dirt
Not count for anything?
Did Melba and Joan Sutherland
Not teach the world to sing?'

'You've never heard of Kingsford-Smith
Or the Sydney Opera House?
I suppose you think 'koala'
Is a breed of Russian mouse!'

'That's Aussie beer you're drinking
Let me put you on the track,
And I'll bet my life that's Aussie wool
In the suit there on your back.'

'Where the hell, then, do you come from
Where they haven't any schools?
And they let their flamin' kids grow up
Such ignoramus fools.'

'I'll have you know', the Yank replied,
That I come from New York town,
And that's in the United States
Renowned the world around.'

'And that's the Land of Liberty
And the home of the brave.
That, Sir, is where I come from!.'
'Never 'eard of it!' said Dave.

Streams and their Names

As Commonwealth Surveyor-General I have a schedule which takes me to all parts of Australia and the world. I particularly enjoyed the letter read a few weeks ago which highlighted some of the idiosyncracies of Australia's stream names.

In my wanderings, both as a surveyor and a map-maker, I have continually been amused and delighted by the imagination our forebears have used in naming places. Indeed, a few of us had good-hearted competitions to find some of the more unusual names. Generally the most unusual were associated with homesteads, but streams and mountains also showed great imagination in their naming.

There are an enormous number of streams named 'Something-or-other Mile' Creek. I have not calculated exactly how many instances there are of the name being used in our 'Master Names File' (a grandiose name for a Gazetteer), but I believe that there would be well over 500 (if not even more). For many years the highest numbered stream I had been able to find was Twenty-Seven Mile Creek. Recently I have found that there is an Eighty Mile Creek near the town of Croydon in far North Queensland.

Without a doubt the most common stream name beyond 'Something-or-other Mile' is Sandy Creek. There are close to 400 instances of the name being used in the 'Master Names File'. The next closest, with over 300 entries, is 'Black something-or-other'—Black Dog, Snake, Gin, Gully and so on and (surprisingly, but highlighting the number of Scots who were early settlers of this country) 'Mac or Mc-someone'. Following these two comes a multitude of names with over 200 entries.. These include Rocky Creek, Middle Creek, Deep Creek (or Gully), Dingo Creek, 'Big something-or-other'—for example, Big Ben, Horse Hill, Rock and (if you can imagine it) Maria and Minnie.

A large number of names are recorded more than 100 times. I think there is an interesting variety in them. Most simply describe the stream or things which are associated with it. They include Boundary Creek (or Gully), Boggy Creek, Camp Creek, Chinaman's Creek, Cedar Creek, Reedy Creek, and, somewhat ominously, Dead something-or-other Creek—for example, Bull, Dog, Horse and Man.

The names I have mentioned are a few of those commonly used. Whilst surveyors were originally instructed to try to find out and use Aboriginal names, it was often quite difficult for them to do so. More recently there has been a revival of interest in Aboriginal names and they are coming into use.

PLATYPUSES

I don't know how we started talking about platypuses—was it talk of training them, or was it Jennifer from Gympie who was concerned about what platypuses would do in a drought and suggested we airlift them, or was it the lady ringing from Brisbane about 'Splash' the platypus? Or did someone write a letter about Healesville Sanctuary, or the work of Harry Burrell? Whatever the reason, it's like many things on *Australia All Over*: I don't know how it started but, like Topsy, it just grew, and we're all the wiser for it.

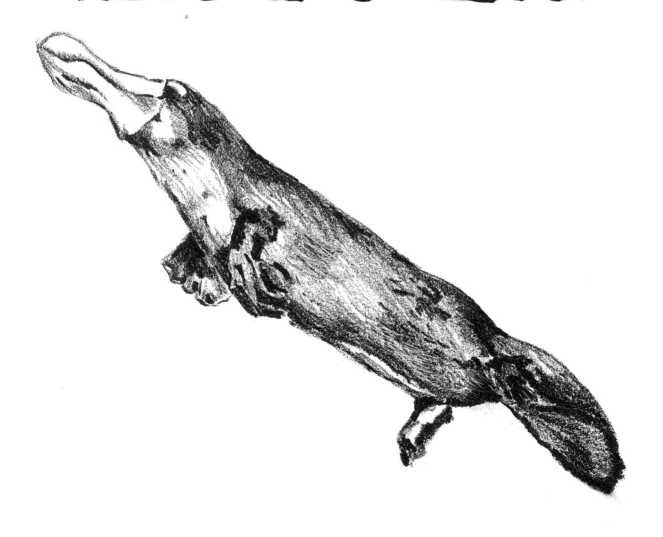

PLATYPUSES

My brother and I lived on a country property nine kilometers south of Barraba. In the school holidays and on weekends we used to explore the countryside, especially the Barraba Creek area.

FROM:
BOB MUNSON
Barraba, NSW

This particular day we decided to go fishing, but first we had to dig some worms for bait. We had a special place to dig the worms under a large willow tree on the banks of Barraba Creek, so on to our horses and down to the willow tree we rode. After digging for about 15 minutes, and not too many worms, we came across a burrow about 150mm (6″) under the surface. About one metre along from where we broke into the burrow we could hear a strange squeaking noise so we decided to investigate. After digging along the burrow to our amazement we came across a nest with two little platypus in it. The nest consisted of some dry grass. After admiring the little fellows, who were about 150mm long, we decided we would have to repair the damage to their home. We found an old sheet of corrugated iron on the bank of the creek and placed it over the trench and covered it with earth and let them be. We used to see the odd platypus along the creek from time to time. It was only in the last few years I realised how significant our discovery was. I have never spoken to any person in the Barraba area who has seen a platypus nest.

For the past fifty-eight years the family of Robert Eadie have believed, and have proof, that he was the first man to keep a platypus alive in captivity. He was the Hon. Curator of the Healesville Sanctuary from 1932-1937. The powers that be at that time gave him permission, if he was able to obtain a platypus, to study its habits.

FROM:
DOROTHY BARLOW

Harry Burrell found a platypus on the banks of the river and gave him to Mr Eadie. 'Splash' was born. Mr Eadie decided that the platypussery erected at the sanctuary was not to his liking so he built his own platypussary at his home, 'Gleneadie'.

Eliza and Robert Eadie now started a wonderful relationship with this platypus. They cared for him twenty-four hours a day until they were sure that he was going to survive. Robert then wrote his book *The Life and Habits of the Platypus* with special reference to Splash. The book is in the National Library in Canberra and I now have one in my possession.

Many visitors from all over the world, including naturalists, visited the Sanctuary, and Splash became a wonder to many people and lived for four and a half years. On his death Robert Eadie received many telegrams from naturalists and interested parties from various parts of the world. Alice Barlow, Robert's daughter, aged ninety-two, lives in South Africa and has these telegrams in her keeping. They will be returned to Australia on her death.

Following the discussion on the plural of platypus (and not being a Greek scholar I will stay out of any platypodean arguments) I thought that the following silly verses might amuse some of your listeners. I apologise for declining (in the grammatical sense) the word as if it was Latin and not Greek based.

I heard a mother platypus
Address her little baby thus
'Now listen to your dear old Mum ,
Or else I'll smack your Platybum;
If you want to do a Platypi
Mark my words most carefully.
Use your china Platypo
Or else you flood the tunnel so.'

This little ditty first appeared in *Urimbirra* (an Aboriginal word meaning 'to take care of or to preserve'), the journal of the Chinchilla Field Naturalists' Club. According to the club's bi-centennial book *Going Bush*, an excellent natural history of the district, the name Chinchilla comes from the Aboriginal word *jinchilla*, the cypress pine.

I was most amused by your comment to the platypus lady re the trouble in finding a platypus drover. These few verses are the result. Please excuse my liberty with the plural for platypuses.

'I know this may seem an impossible dream,
But, let us pause for a moment and think,
If the rivers run dry, Ornithorhynchus will die,
And around Gympie they will be extinct'.

Ian replied, 'Your have me on side,
I'll give your scheme the once over.
The trouble you see, is going to be,
In finding a platypus drover.'

THE VARIETY CLUB'S REDEX BASH

Catching up with the Redex Bash in 1988, Ian was near Lake Eyre, then at Tibooburra airport and with Paul Jennings. Ian also broadcast from the Fitzroy River Lodge at Fitzroy Crossing and performed with an Aboriginal band.

In the Northern Territory

Ian stopped at the Devils Marbles en route for Newcastle Waters where he broadcast in May 1988 during the Last Great Cattle Drive. He interviewed a dozer driver on the highway between Alice Springs and Tennant Creek and the guitar came into play at the motel at Marla Bore.

CARNIVAL OF FLOWERS

Broadcasting from Toowoomba in September 1988, Ian opened the Carnival of Flowers and later talked to some of the local cricketers at the Toowoomba Shopping Mall.

BRISBANE...BOTANIC GARDENS AAO CONCERT

Australia All Over was broadcast from Brisbane's Botanic Gardens in November 1989 . . . At the AAO Concert Ron and Joy Lakim from Toowoomba were photographed 'washing chooks' and performers included the Wynnum Harmonica Band.

PLATYPUSES

When Lake Burley Griffin filled in 1964, the ACT Water Police was set up as a branch of what was then the ACT Police. The Water Police naturally acquired a launch in which they could patrol their aquatic beat, and for some obscure reason decided they would like to give it a classical name. They asked the Professor of Classics at the Australian National University to suggest a name and he proposed they call the police launch the *Platypus*, saying that he considered it an appropriate name for three reasons:

- it was derived from classical Greek;
- it was particularly suitable for something serving the national, capital, since the platypus is uniquely Australian; and
- like the police, the platypus functioned both in the water and on land.

So the police launch was duly named *Platypus*. It was only some time later that it was pointed out to the police that the professor had played a little joke on them, because the meaning of 'platypus' in classical Greek is 'flatfoot'—a fourth reason for considering the name appropriate for something belonging to the police! So even though the joke was on them, the police kept the name and the *Platypus* continued to patrol the waters of Lake Burley Griffin for many years.

When I was living in North Queensland in the late 1950s-early 1960s, I recall a trip to the Millstream Falls on the Atherton Tableland. Early one sunny afternoon I had the great joy of watching two platypuses playing in the pool at the foot of the falls. It was a real thrill. The falls were remote and relatively untouched in those days.

On another occasion I visited Herberton, a tin-mining town where the huge dredges were ripping apart the streams where the platypuses lived. A resident there told me she knew of a fur coat owned by the wife of one of the senior mine staff. It was made from 161 pelts of platypus! Even in those days I was horrified at the wanton slaughter of a unique species.

Please keep up your efforts on behalf of the preservation of our heritage.

As we call more than one sheep, sheep, and as we call more than one fish, fish, may I suggest the simplest plural for platypus be 'platypus'? This is simple, logical and sounds fine in a sentence: 'There are two platypus in our lake.' 'Platypus are unique to Australia.'

To use 'platypuses' as the plural not only sounds cumbersome and contrived (as does Joneses and Coleses for Jones and Coles) but it immediately raises a spelling problem: is it to be platypuses or platypusses or even platypussies?

No, I think platypus for both singular and plural is very simple and so would be very acceptable.

Might I also make another couple of points? If, as some suggest, the plural is 'platypi' (the Latin style plural which I believe to be unacceptable because of the Greek origin of the roots) then the correct pronunciation would be 'platypee'. If you want to pronounce it 'platypie' then the spelling would need to be 'platypae' and this would be most incorrect in Latin.

What say we try 'platypus' and stick with it?

No-one would believe that such a simple problem could engage so many minds and produce so many differences of opinions. But, just as you love trains, I love language.

With regard to the platypus controversy over its plural, herewith my two bob's worth for the record, in verse:

FROM:
JACK OGLE
Tuncurry, NSW

This English language
Drives me nuts,
With all its wherefores
Ifs and buts.
If several mouse
Are rightly mice,
Wouldn't it
Be really nice
If a couple of platypus
Were simply—'platypice'?

I listen to your program every week and really enjoy hearing the diversity of subjects and people and places.

Recently you have been talking about platypus and I thought you might be interested in the following.

Concerning platypuses or platypi—in David Fleay's book *Paradoxical Platypus—Hobnobbing with Duckbills* the following paragraph occurs.

> The correct plural of platypus still remains a matter of debate. Platypi is disqualified because of the incompatibility of a Latin plural with a Greek noun. Platypodes, though correct, is awkward and unwieldy, and would probably never find its way into the vernacular. So why not, for the sake of popularity and clarity, refer to a platypus in the singular and platypuses in the plural? Most people do this, and there is no room for doubt as to what they mean.

FROM:
VALERIE CHAPMAN
Croydon, Victoria

My interpretation of this is that you cannot put a Latin 'i' on a Greek platypus.

FROM:
NEIL O'SULLIVAN
Nedlands
Western Australia

A keen listener of *Australia All Over*, it's not often that I can speak with professional competence about the subjects discussed on the show, as I teach Classics, ie. Latin and Ancient Greek! But the area is always relevant to our lives, not least because so many of the words in English derive from these languages.

Your segment this morning on the platypus provides a case in point. The plural form was given a few times as 'platypi'; this is simply false pedantry (being a genuine pedant myself, I can usually spot impostors!) Let me explain the mistake.

Many Latin words end in -us, and form a plural in -i (eg. *terminus*); equivalent Greek nouns end in -os with a plural in -oi, although these are often Latinized in English (eg. *hippopotamus*, which has an -os ending in Greek),

However, *platypus* does not fall into this category, for the -us ending does not represent a Greek -os with a plural in -oi. Rather, -pus stands for the Greek *pous* (foot), which has a plural *podes*. So, if one wants to use a form other than the obvious *platypuses*, one should really say *platypodes*, although I've never seen this in print.

However, dictionaries give *octopuses* as well as *octopodes* on the same principle. Admittedly, the *Macquarie Dictionary* has *platypi*, but that work does not inspire confidence in its scholarship.

I fear all of this might be out of place on your excellent show, surely the glory of Australian radio.

I am no scholar but I have listened to the discussion re that unique and quite delightful water creature, the platypus, with much amusement. The pedants are out in force mixing their Latin and Greek roots every which away. I did seriously think of calling several of these appealing animals 'platycats' but have decided to change my mind. In future if I am ever in the position to see more than one splashing in a river I shall declare in a very loud and excited voice 'There's a platypus—and there's another one!!'
PS A friend once saw a platypus in the creek that ran through his property. He raced into the house calling 'I've seen a hippopotamus—I've seen a hippopotamus!'

From:
VONNE HUTCHINSON
Healesville
Victoria

PLATYPUSES

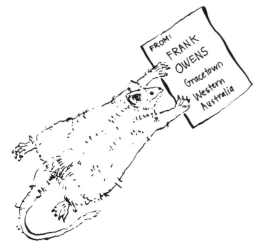

I've been so amused by the platypus or platypii debate that I just had to transform delight into verse. Cheers—hope you like it, mate!

Confused

I'm confused by Greek expression
Or even ancient Latin,
I'd hate to think a platypii
Was something that I'd sat on!

Perhaps a brace of platypus
Might be the best expression,
I'm getting rather tongue tied
On your Sunday morning session.

I've listened with amusement
As some debate the plural,
Of platypodes or platypii
In my seclusion rural.

I know you'll reach consensus
But I thought I'd pen a word,
I'm agog with all the knowledge
On your program that I've heard!

Some can't know for certain
With Greek or ancient Latin,
That platypodes or platypii
Ain't something that they've sat on.

I wish to enter the lists on the matter of platypus. *The Australasian Dictionary* of 1898 is very helpful on the subject. In 1799 the monotreme was named Platypus Anatinus by Shaw. However, six years earlier, the generic name platypus (meaning 'broad foot') had been allotted to a species of beetle. So, in 1800, in accordance with the rules of zoological nomenclature, the monotreme gave way to the beetle and was renamed Ornithorhynchus. But the animal's popular name of platypus prevailed in Australia despite Lydekker's recommendation in 1894 that it would be 'preferable to discard the Anglicised term Duck-billed Platypus in favour of the simpler Duck-bill or Duck-Mole. (It was also known as a Water-Mole.)

Clearly, the matter of the plural formation of the scientific word 'platypus', which is modern Latin adopted from the Greek, should only concern those faced with two or more beetles of the genus platypus. Our furry, duck-billed, web-footed, beaver-tailed monotreme, on the other hand, has its own Latinised scientific name—Ornithorhyncus—and, presumably, we have no difficulty with that plural.

Platypus, as the editor of *The Australasian Dictionary* noted, having become 'by long usage the ordinary vernacular name, is the one by which the animal will always be known in Australian popular language.' In short, platypus, in its vernacular use, can take the simple plural by adding 'es', without upsetting the classical scholars; and if buses, walruses, terminuses, campuses, hippopotamuses and mongooses don't cause us any anguish, why should platypuses?

I thought you might be interested in my encounter with David Fleay.

In April 1947, not long after the war ended and when it was still difficult to get across the Pacific, I travelled with my parents from Brisbane to Boston on an American freighter. It carried ten passengers including Mr and Mrs Fleay, who were taking three platypuses to the Bronx Zoo. Up to that point, before air transport was as sophisticated as it is today, no platypuses had survived endeavours to export them to overseas zoos. A platypus hut had been constructed on the ship's forward cargo deck simulating as far as possible the animals' natural habitat. A mammoth supply of fresh and frozen worms was carried as their food supply.

There was little occupation for the passengers and the health and welfare of the platypuses, called Penelope, Cecil and Betty Hutton, became our major interest. An invitation to see the platypuses, usually in the evening when they were awake, was like an invitation to Buckingham Palace. When Betty Hutton got a grass seed stuck in her nose it was a major disaster. There was high drama when the supply of fresh worms ran out and our important passengers refused to eat frozen ones. This necessitated an unscheduled call at Pitcairn Island where a supply of fresh worms was picked up after the ship radioed ahead a request for the Islanders to dig for worms like mad.

The platypuses, thanks to Mr Fleay's great care, reached Boston safely, and when last seen by me were being loaded on to road transport for the trip to the Bronx. I understand they were successfully established there and lived for several years.

The Steps at Newtown Station

I love you so, though you refuse
To note my admiration,
I'll always know the days you use,
The steps at Newtown Station.

You first came here, quite long ago,
A little girl aged seven,
And every year I watched you grow,
Till soon you were eleven.

You turned eighteen, and blossomed out,
To add to my elation,
And paint the scene, around about,
The steps at Newtown Station.

If I were free, I'd take your hand,
And seek your adulation,
And turn the key to wonderland,
A magic destination.

To win your heart, undying love,
I'd always be professing,
We'd never part, for from above,
Would flow the choicest blessing.

But fate has deemed it otherwise,
Your charms I shall be missing.
Although I've dreamed, I have no eyes,
Nor lips you could be kissing.

I've lost my style, and feel run down,
And hardly fit for flirting,
I never smile, but wear a frown,
When all those feet are hurting.

You can't love me, I understand,
I'm not of God's creation,
I'll always be, cement and sand
The steps at Newtown Station.

The Magic Ring

That little bit of trivia on last Sunday's show got me in. Before you could say 'bottoms up' I had the wife's wedding ring off, tied a piece of string to it and went around the house chasing the family off all the chairs in the place. I found to my surprise that your informant was correct: the wedding ring starts to move of its own free will, round and round for females and back and forth for males.

I immediately began to wonder if this could be turned to our advantage. Could we suspend our wives from the jib of a mobile crane and drive around the country? Would they start going around in circles when we were over a golden reef? The possibilities are endless. However, I have confined myself to a short verse:

I heard on Macca's Sunday show
A snippet that I didn't know.
A tale of how a wedding ring
Suspended by a piece of string,
Could tell us whether Charles or Claire
Had sat upon a certain chair.
But Macca said, 'Well, strike me blue,
I don't believe that story's true'.

Well, look, old mate, I tried it out
On men and women, slim and stout:
On chairs that held a Dick or Jack
The ring swings straight from front to back.
But if it's Fanny's chair you've found
It circles round and round and round.
So, bottoms of the world, beware -
You've left your mark upon the chair.

FROM: BILL GLASSON, Clifton, Queensland

CHRISTMAS

One of my favourite *Australia All Over* programs was on Christmas Day 1988. It was a ripper, I felt. It was the first one I'd done live on Christmas morning and there was the feeling of Christmas about it, with people calling in from all over the place. I had Christmas poems, Christmas songs, and there was really a spirit of caring and sharing right around Australia. The monks from New Norcia in Western Australia rang in to tell us how they spent Christmas Day; other listeners told us they were going to play cricket, and Roger Oxley wrote about Christmas bush. All in all, it was just a great program.

Bill Smith's letter from Port Elliott is just a ripper, too

CHRISTMAS

This is a Christmas story you might like to use. I grew up in Quirindi, a small town near Tamworth. Through many years my late mother dealt with a Chinese storekeeper named Fred Nightjoy. He traded as Sing Sing & Co. The business has long since ceased to exist but I don't know whether or not Fred is still living. He was one of nature's hentlemen and, with his family, was well respected in the community. He was also unusual in that he made it a practice to give a Christmas present to regular customers and, in my mother's case, this usually took the form of a bottle of fruit juice and a bottle of sherry. If Fred had any shortcoming, it was perhaps his command of the English language. One year his Christmas present gave even more enjoyment than he might have expected. My mother was about sixty at the time, and that fact is relevant, because her Christmas order was accompanied by a brown paper parcel that appeared to contain the usual bottles of fruit cup and sherry, but on the wrapping Fred had written—'To Mrs Hannaford From Fred and Wishing you the Confinement of the Season'!

FROM:
B. A. HANNAFORD
Mudgee
NSW

I'm wondering how many of your listeners are put off by the myth of a white, cold Christmas with which we are bombarded in every shopping centre in this warm country at the hottest time of year—the artificial snow is really annoying me this year, not to mention the tinny strains of sleighbells and reindeer-related carols over the p.a. systems. Surely after 200 years we have developed some Australian Christmas traditions!

Two things spring immediately to my mind. The first is related very much to living in Brisbane—the red and green traditional Christmas colours are confirmed for me—not in fir trees and red berries—but in the beautiful spreading poinciana trees that put on such a magnificent show in December. As soon as they begin to bloom I know that it's time to start sending Christmas cards and wrap up gifts.

FROM:
ANNETTE DEANS
Wishard
Queensland

Was feeling inspired to write a Christmas poem and thought you might like to hear it.

FROM:
B. J. CRANE
Willetton, Western Australia

I know it's close to Christmas
For the days are that much longer
And the nights are getting warmer
While the bushfire's smoke smells stronger.

It must be close to Christmas
All the magpie's young are flying

And the sun is getting stronger
While the meadow grass is dying.

It surely must be Christmas
When the eastwind greets the dawn
And the Christmas Bush is blooming
While all the sheep are shorn.

I know it's close to Christmas
For the postie brings us greetings
And lots of cards from far off lands
Showing snow filled, candlelight meetings.

It must be close to Christmas
For the sky is raincloud free
And joy and laughter fill the air
As children dress up their tree.

It surely must be Christmas
For nature has its own way
Of telling us it's Christmas time
With its beauty 'on display'.

For now that it is Christmas
Let us take some time to recall
Those boundless gifts, so freely given
By our Lord to us, one and all.

FROM:
MARY TANNER
Indigo Valley
Victoria

This morning we heard 'I Made a Hundred in the Back Yard at Mum's' and then at the end of the program you advised us to play cricket today rather than drive on the roads.

We are writing to tell you that our family has been playing cricket on Christmas Day now for thirteen years. True to the song, we play at Mum's, in the side yard rather than the back yard, with the outfielders stationing themselves on the other side of the electric fence in an adjoining paddock.

We use a twelve-gallon drum at the batter's end and a four-gallon drum at the bowler's end. We always bowl from the same end. We don't follow the rule book too closely; in fact most of us don't know the rules, and allowance is always made for either advanced age or extreme youth so that everyone can participate. Three generations take part in the game.

When I was overseas on Christmas Day some years ago the rest of the family lazily sat around saying: 'If Mary was here we'd be playing cricket. I suppose we'd better get out and play.'

We all have a lot of fun; in fact, mirth and hilarity are the order of the day and it is very much a Tanner family tradition for Christmas Day. Should you wish to visit us on this day you'd be welcome to join in.

Aunt Molly

'Twas in the supermarket Ollie met his Aunty Molly,
Busy with her Christmas shopping, helped by Uncle Wally,
With hams and chooks and bottles and some vegies and a cauli,
She walked along the aisle while Uncle Wally pushed the trolley.

Aunt Molly smiled and said, 'G'day. How are you going, Ollie?
Christmas time is coming, it's the season to be jolly.
We're going to decorate the house with streamers, lights and holly.'
Ollie walked beside while Uncle Wally pushed the trolley.

Aunt Molly said, 'I don't know what to get for little Polly.'
Ollie thought a while and said, 'Why not a little dolly?
And a great big Christmas stocking full of games and things and lollies?'
Said Uncle Wally, 'We are going to need another trolley.'

'It's raining,' said Aunt Molly, 'and I didn't bring the brolly.'
Then Uncle Wally came up with a pretty volley.
'Aunt Molly has no brolly, Ollie. Golly, that is folly.'
Aunt Molly walked ahead while Uncle Wally pushed the trolley.

When you are Christmas shopping, should you chance to meet Aunt Molly,
With a dolly in a trolley pushed along by Uncle Wally,
And hams and chooks and holly, bottles, vegies and a cauli,
Please wish them Merry Christmas, for they really are quite jolly.

FROM:
RON STRAHAN
~
Sofala
NSW

Continuing on the theme of trees and shrubs mentioned in John Broomhall's Wild and Free, I thought it would be appropriate for your Christmas program to talk about Christmas bush.

Like most common plant names, the term Christmas bush refers to various kinds of plants in different regions and states.

In the Sydney area Christmas bush is a small tree growing naturally in infertile soils of forest areas and gullies. Its flowers are a creamy colour, but the parts surrounding the flower give it the pink/red colour that makes it so attractive. This particular plant is interesting because it is a remnant from a period some fifty million years ago when rainforests extended across southern Australia and it is one of the few plants to

FROM:
ROGER OXLEY
Deniliquin, NSW

have adapted and survived to the low fertility sandy soils around Sydney.

The Victorian Christmas bush is related to the mint bushes and is more of a shrub than a tree. In summer it has masses of snowy white flowers and can be found along creek banks in moist gullies near Melbourne, and the Dandenongs. Young saplings of this shrub are highly prized by small boys for making fishing rods.

The South Australian Christmas bush is yet another species called by this common name. It is a densely branched shrub, or small tree, quite spiny, and has numerous creamy flowers during summer. This Christmas bush grows in almost all parts of the state but is more common in the south-east of South Australia, especially in association with mallee.

If you live in the west then you have the Western Australian Christmas tree. It's a shrub or small tree growing to about seven metres with numerous attractive orange and yellow flowers during summer and is found growing on well-drained soils from the Murchison River right around to the Bight.

This tree is parasitic on the roots of other plants and is related to the mistletoe. Mistletoe and kisses are just as synomous with Christmas as are roast turkey and plum pudding—why not plant one on your missus this morning!

Please find enclosed a copy of the experiences of three Darwinians during the morning that cyclone Tracy devastated Darwin. We often hear you mention Darwin and cyclone Tracy.

The Long Night

Date: Christmas Day, 1974
Place: Casuarina Hospital Construction Site, Tiwi, Darwin, NT
Residence: 7m, steel frame aluminium caravan.

12.01 am   George (forty-six years) and Christine (11 years) cutting out Christmas decorations while Joyce (forty-four years) is making late supper and drinks as she has just arrived home from her job at a Darwin hotel. Joyce is uptight as she has just walked 1km to the caravan in very strong wind of about 90 kph and driving rain.

1.00 am   Power has failed and the caravan is suffering severe buffeting from wind and rain, sand and small articles of flying debris are hammering the caravan like bullets.

1.20 am   Continuous buffeting by the wind has broken the airconditioner from its fixture and torn the rear ceiling vent away. All three are feverishly tossing the contents of the overhead cupboards on to the floor in an attempt to lower the caravan's centre of gravity.

1.25 am   The front ceiling vent is now torn away and the caravan steel tie-downs begin to break.

1.30 am   The caravan is now lifting up and down from its mountings

by about half a metre; the feeling inside is like a boat in a heavy sea.
1.35 am   The caravan is blown over onto its roof and some windows are shattered.
1.40 am   The caravan rolls over and over for about two hundred metres then comes to a rocking halt on its wheels for about five minutes. During this short lull all three check with each other for serious injuries; George has a dislocated shoulder.
1.45 am   The caravan starts rolling again, travels about another two hundred metres and comes to a sudden crashing halt against a partly constructed concrete block wall. The wind is so strong that it is impossible to check each other and it is so noisy that communication is out of the question; it is just a matter of huddling down in what is left of the caravan for what seems an eternity. There just seems no end to the howling, shrieking and hammering of the wind, rain, sand and debris.
5.30 am   The wind is still very strong but easing, and they can talk to each other at last and check out each other's problems. George and Joyce are unable to move but are coherent. Christine appears to have fared the best but is slightly hysterical.
6.00 am   It is still blowing and raining, but visibility is sufficient to check each other in some detail. Christine is mobile, George is pinned under the refrigerator and cannot move, Joyce has the deep freezer across her upper body and cannot move and can only talk with great effort; it's now all up to Christine. George asks her to go for help but, when she stands up and looks out at her surroundings, she tells the sad tale that there is absolutely nothing standing or moving as far as she can see and that is about one kilometre. There are no buildings standing, very few trees and of those only the trunks are there; all branches, leaves and even the grass on the ground are gone. All is blown and sandblasted into oblivion. There is no roof and no walls above about one metre on the caravan, and only a small section of steel frame is swaying in the wind.
6.30 am   Christine has removed the refrigerator from George and has found a strip of curtain, made a sling for his arm and propped him against the remains of a bunk. She then attempts to free Joyce from under the freezer, but the electrical flex attached to it is wrapped around George's lower body and something has to be found to cut it. Luck is with her—a carving knife is miraculously at George's feet. The cord is cut and Joyce is freed. She is very distressed and unable to move much and is coughing up blood. The three try to make themselves as comfortable as possible and hope that help will come soon.
8.00 am   Wayne (Joyce's son) and Cheryl (Wayne's friend) arrive from Mindil Beach (Darwin City) where they have left their wrecked caravan to come and see how things are at Tiwi. They are not injured, but are

badly shaken and tell the story that the whole of the city and suburbs are almost wiped out, and it has taken them from first light to drive the twelve kilometres out to Tiwi. They first carry George and Joyce to their car, Christine is able to walk. The drive to Darwin Hospital is an absolute nightmare in itself. The roads are strewn with all manner of obstacles: parts of houses, roofs, walls, furniture, fences, trees, cars, telephone and light poles, wires and many other things that once were essential to sustain a thriving city of 43,000 people.

9.30 am   Darwin Hospital has no roof; it is raining heavily; the injured are there in dozens and more arriving each minute. The staff are very severely handicapped but are coping as best as circumstances permit. The seriously injured require specialised and urgent attention, the not so serious also require attention, and, above all, everyone requires 'tender loving care', and that rare commodity is freely and willingly given.

12.00 noon   George is now in a ward with the seriously injured, he has a fractured spine and is paralysed from the waist down. His left shoulder has been dislocated and the head of the humerus has multiple fractures, not to mention three broken toes and a multitude of minor cuts and bruises. Joyce has three fractured ribs, and again a multitude of minor cuts and bruises. She is classified among the walking injured, but no hospital accommodation is available. Christine has been found to have lost the heel of her left foot and has a severe laceration across her buttock, and minor lacerations and bruises. These were all great tragedies in themselves, but the greatest tragedy was yet to come when they were evacuated south from this scene of almost total devastation and the reality that they had lost all their material possessions had to be faced.

Aftermath: Some say 'charity begins at home' but George, Joyce and Christine will tell you that 'charity' took on a new significance after Tracy; that charity came from almost every person they met for many months after. All three returned to Darwin within months and re-established themselves as best they could, but their memory of Christmas Day, 1974, is as vivid now as it was then.

FROM:
BILL SMITH
Port Elliot
South Australia

In 1953 we were dairy farming at Narbethong on the Acheron River fifty miles north-east of Melbourne—truly God's Own Country. We were a city family and I was delighted to be asked to play Father Christmas at the school at Buxton, our nearest township. I felt we were newcomers being accepted into the community, and besides I'd always wanted to be Santa.

My instructions were to pick up and change into the uniform at the Buxton Hotel and arrive at the school at 2.30pm, so we took the hood off the Land Rover, hosed it down, put on the suit etc as arranged, and with my wife driving and me standing in the back we arrived right on time with much ho! ho! hoing! There was the pub, then the local hall and then the school, and as we drew near the teacher came out and said 'Go back! Go back! The children haven't finished their party yet! We'll call you when we're ready!'

Well, there we were in the middle of nowhere dressed in Father Christmas rig, and the only sane thing to do was to take off the whiskers and head for the pub and pass the time as best we could at the bar. When the call eventually came to make an appearance I was in a party mood, to put it mildly, and got a great reception. There were about forty children at the school at that time and I had to give out the presents and take orders for toys from each youngster, and I had a ball. It seemed to me that I did all right except for trying to kiss the divinity teacher (an elderly spinster) and getting knocked back, and I returned home still glowing. However, on sobering up I realised I'd been a bit over-generous, especially to one boy who'd asked me for an electric train, so I rang his father and apologised for putting him in a spot, but he wasn't upset as they had no electricity so that let him out!

Next day I was getting some petrol at the Buxton Garage and I said to the bloke, 'Gawd! I got a bit carried away at the school party yesterday and promised young Leon an electric train.' He said, 'That's nothing! You promised my kid a pony!!' I think he put some horse manure on the back step and said that it must have got away, but I was never asked to be Santa again!

FROM
MARGARET WICKHAM
Karara, Queensland

Singing Bulls

Our daughter, aged fifteen, is learning to play trombone as part of her music subject for Year 10. When she comes home (she is at boarding school) and practises her trombone, we are entertained by our bulls (Poll Hereford, of course—the cultured ones). One sings tenor, one bass, and the young one yodels (I think). As soon as our daughter starts to play they come from all corners of the paddock to breast the house-yard fence. When they are in full voice it's not easy to tell who is singing (or playing) out of tune.

FROM
ROSS HENRY
New Norfolk, Tasmania

I dreamt I watched a footie game

I dreamt I watched a footie game
One winter afternoon
A darn good game it surely was;
It finished all too soon.

But as I left the crowded ground
In the best of all good humours
I couldn't help but wonder why
They called themselves the Pumas.

Now, the puma is a lovely beast,
I wouldn't wish it ill
But it doesn't live where we all live.
And I'm sure it never will.
(Of course, there could be one or two
In Melbourne or Taronga zoo.)

And in this dream the other team
Described themselves in Spanish.
Bronchos was the name they chose . . .
. . . It helps our culture vanish.

One night I hope to have more dreams
Of matches and of clubs:
The Koalas and the Shearers
Or the Bookies and the Pubs.

The Stockmen down the Wirraways,
The Redbacks beat the Ringers;
The Wobegongs and the Drovers tie
In a ladder of humdingers.

And then the Ironbarks trot out
To battle with the Taipans
The Diggers roast the Funnelwebs
From the fire to the frypans.

So 'carn the Barramundies
Up there the Cockatoos,
You flamin' beaut Rosellas;
The Bullockies can't lose.'

And here's another first-class match
The Troopers play the Miners
The winner meets the Larrikins
A team there's none as fine as.

The Stubbies thrash the Yabbies
The Gum Leaves trounce the Wattles
And on that great Grand Final night
The club's awash with bottles.

All this is sheer fantasy —
Imaginary games.
But . . . Jeez . . . they're all around us!!
There're stacks of Aussie names!!

Another word before I go
And I bet my mole-skin trousers
It could only be in this land of mine
That the Ratbags play the Wowsers.

74

GUMBOOTS

Originally a Scottish air about the work of weavers, 'Gumboots' was taken up by Billy Connolly for the 'Welly' song. Then Fred Dagg in New Zealand did the 'Gumboots' song, and I thought we ought to do an Australian version. We have great fun with this at concerts. If you ever attend an *Australia All Over* concert you must, repeat must, bring a pair of gumboots, preferably decorated. Near the end of the concerts the stage is invaded by forty or fifty people dancing the 'Gumboots' song. An amazing sight!

GUMBOOTS

This gumboot story is true and concerns friends of mine who shall remain nameless.

A few years ago they left Sydney, the two of them, to make a trip around Australia. The husband said 'You can't take this and you can't take that, we have to conserve space, we have to carry water, fuel and food, we don't need two pairs of gumboots—if we get bogged one of us still has to stay in the vehicle', so they took just the one pair.

Naturally, a few weeks later, they found themselves bogged and it was time to get out the gumboots, which they did. They were both for the left foot!

FROM: RAYNEE BIRD
Wyangala Dam, NSW

FROM: ROBERT PRIOR
Mount Eliza
Victoria

Recently I heard you play the 'Gumboot Song'. Such was my mood at the time that I could not continue with the job in hand (fixing the lawnmower), so I retreated to the kitchen, put the kettle on and jotted down the accompanying poem.

I know you have an in-depth appreciation of gumboots and will understand where I'm coming from in regard to my lost friends.

My Green Boots

Do you know I've lost me gumboots?
They were the best you've ever seen,
Cut from the bottom of me waders
And coloured khaki green.

Most gumboots that I've ever owned
Were stiff and hard when worn,
But these old boots were just like gloves
And for my feet were born.

How can you lose ya gumboots?
It's not as though they're small
And they're always falling over
When you leave them in the hall.

Or out on the verandah
If their scent is sweet and strong
Where ya Mum would always throw them
Out there where they belong.

I used to keep them in my car
In case I'd find a place,
Where long wet grass or sticky mud,
Would city shoes efface

I've looked at other gumboots
In shops around the towns
Sitting in store windows,
Like rows and rows of clowns

At Elders and Dalgetys
Or the Co-op down the line
But haven't seen a gumboot
As beautiful as mine

I once tried on a pair of boots
At a shop in a country town
But felt like a bloody traitor
I'd let my green boots down

So I left the shop without them
And still no boots I own
I sit at night and wonder
If my boots are all alone

I'll never find another boot
To fit my feet so sweet
But while I'm faithful to them ,
I'll always have wet feet

So if you ever see these boots
That have a soul and heart,
Please write and tell me where they are
And keep us not apart.

At a dinner party the other night we got to discussing 'Australia All Over' and the 'Gumboots Song' was mentioned. One of our guests said she had her own gumboots story:

While her husband was on night work she was sleeping alone— and, incidentally, au natural—when she looked up and saw a huge huntsman spider on the ceiling above the bed.

She decided she would sweep it down on to the white carpet so she could see it to suck it up with the vacuum cleaner, so she put on her gumboots in case it attacked her feet once it was down. I would like listeners to imagine a well-endowed lady, clad only in a pair of rubber boots, using a long handled broom to do battle with a spider.

Anyway, it seems the spider didn't want to come down, and so it hung from its thread half way. She then went and got the vacuum cleaner and sucked it up from mid-air. All this was repeated in mime by our guest, although I hasten to add she remained fully clad for the performance on this occasion.

That's not the end of the story. Having got the spider into the vacuum cleaner she became worried that it would get out again.

At this stage, her husband chipped in and said that when he arrived home he sat for a good half hour trying to write down the possible reasons why at 3.30 am he should find the family vacuum cleaner abandoned in the middle of the back garden.

Eventually he gave up and woke his wife to ask.

The people who fell about laughing at this dinner party would be delighted if you could play the 'Gumboots Song' and dedicate it to 'Louise'.

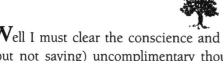

Well I must clear the conscience and come clean—I've been thinking (but not saying) uncomplimentary thoughts about 'gumboots' for quite some time—more so when I hear the much-loved (not by myself) 'Gumboot Song'. However, as my Dad would say, 'The day will come'. And it did—in the big flood that hit us last month, a never-to-be-forgotten rush of waters that left half the western towns 'sodden' to say the least, and stunned. Since we are more or less on the border of the semi-arid line and famous for our big drys and excessive heat, this flood was something for which most of us (like me) weren't prepared. I had no gumboots—well, I did have an old pair from way back when, which unfortunately I'd rather crudely reduced to half-mast, to reduce not the height but the weight.

FROM:
ENID BRYAN
Barcaldine
Queensland

However, they proved to be more of a hindrance than a help when the water got deep enough to ride over the tops. So, I went to the shop to buy a pair of galoshes. The shop assistant said 'Oh, you mean gumboots! Well, there you are!'; but they were only a little short-legged overshoe, pretty but useless, and definitely not the gumboot in the song. So looks like I'm up for a pair. I can't afford to be caught digging trenches without me gumboots!

FROM: J. W. WATT
Briagolong
Victoria

No Return

Out on the back verandah I lay where I was flung;
The toil of day was over, the ev'ning just begun;
Inside was warmth and laughter, the sounds and smells of food,
But out on the verandah there was a different mood.

Along with all the others, from large to very small
I lay unloved, discarded, forgotten, by the wall.
But soon I'll have my moment of glory and applause,
'Cos at the Gumboot Throwing my turn will come, because

Once I am tossed and airborne I'll wander from the track,
I'm not a ruddy boomerang . . . *this gumboot won't come back*!

Gum Boots

The best boots of all are the Gums,
They've toes, feet and heels, but no tums,
They're ideal for cricket,
Played on a wet wicket
Down in the backyard at Mum's.

Without them, where would we be?
In mullock, right up to the knee,
They make your feet pong,
So it says in the song,
On *Australia All Over* (vol.three).

FROM:
KEITH GRAVER
Howrah, Tasmania

Me Gumboots

They shield you from the prickles
And the pig and cattle bogs;
They're missiles for the 28s
And amorous courting mogs;
They're containers for nasturtiums,
Water dishes for the dogs.

They may not smell of roses
When I rightly prise them off,
But my gumboots are more precious
Than the 'Iris' of Van Gogh.

FROM:
D. HAMILTON
Northam, Western Australia

Gumboots—joyous accessories of drought-breaking rain. I love the clomping sloshing of my 'seven league boots'. Gumboots mean the earth has been washed and slaked, and will wake rejuvenated tomorrow morning, clothed in palest green. Grass will grow, crops flourish, and some of the lines will leave our faces. Gumboots!

FROM:
JANET GOODYEAR
Morven
Queensland

Gumboots—God bless 'em!
Queensland's Wet—warm humid days—gutters full and rushing—grassy areas saturated—puddles and mud galore. Enjoying daily walks with gumboots and dog—acting like kids—paddling—splashing—sloshing

FROM:
JUDITH LANCASTER
Point Vernon
Queensland

along the way. Who cares about apparent loss of sanity? Having too
much fun in me gumboots!

My Old Dad's Friends

They sit by the fire each night
Beside my old Dad's chair,
They're with him every hour
Through weather foul and fair.
Silent, strong and trusty,
Part them, who would dare?
Man's best friend? Well no, not quite,
Just Dad's old dirty gumboots,
A pair, one left, one right.

FROM: SHIRLEY JONES
∞
Croydon Victoria

My Gumboots

I love a sunburnt country
I love my gumboots too
They've been with me to Streaky Bay
Pine Creek and Kakadu

I love my smelly gumboots
But what an awful sight
That's why my family make me put
Them buggers out at night.

FROM: ANNE SMALLWOOD
Brighton, South Aust.

Why You Are Never Dressed Unless You've Got Your Gumboots On!

Bull ants, snakes and dogs that bite,
Hoofbeats sudden in the night,
Next door's ram caught in the wire,
Bush to check in case of fire,
Sodden paddocks, wilful cattle,
Country life's a running battle!
Nightie, ballgown or bikini
Tiara, 'Kubra or my beanie,
I'm not worried, shy or stressed -
With gumboots I am fully dressed!

FROM: BETTY ROBERTS
Exeter
Tasmania

GUMBOOTS

FROM:
DIANNE GREGSON
Turramurra, NSW

I am a city slicker
With a routine, cut and dry,
But country places I love to visit
I tell you, that's no lie.

We pack up all the camping gear
What we take is such a hoot!
And even though the car is full
We always take the boots.

They are an essential part of camping
As important as a flash light
You can wear them when nature calls you
In the middle of the night.

You can wear them to go fishing
You can wear them when you please
Or simply when it's raining
For they do prevent a sneeze!

You get a sense of pleasure
When a puddle you traverse
While other feet are soaking
And the water they do curse.

There's a unique kind of odour
Only gumboots can create
And it often is mistaken
For last week's smelly bait.

And when I'm back at home again
I wear them in the garden
For though my feet may sweat all day
There's no chance they will harden.

Though this footwear may cause a stir
And not be the latest fashion
My favourite old black gumboots and I
Have a special kind of passion.

Ode to Gumboots

Whether drenching old ewes—or
Cleaning up the shed floor,
Maybe collecting mallee roots,
In our all important gumboots;

FROM:
JANET BYRNE
Lameroo, South Aust.

GUMBOOTS

We feel kinda smart and regal,
All proper-like and legal -
Real regular country coots,
In our yellow'n'black gumboots.
Sure—materially we're poor -
Poverty's knockin' at our door,
But we couldn't care two hoots -
We love life—in our gumboots!
What could be more exciting'?
(When we're not actually fightin')
An' about our jobs, we've scooted,
'n' relaxed—at home—unbooted,
'e looks at me with praise,
'n' says that romantic phrase -
'You've worked just great, Toots,
In your brand new gum boots!'
An' I looks back at him -
Now, not so young and slim,
An' I assess his attributes -
Includin' his trusty gumboots!
Into the future, together, we gaze,
What's ahead is all a haze!
When we join angels 'n' their lutes -
Sure hope we're wearin' our gumboots!

I like wearing my gumbies when I am in the bush. The snakes and crocodiles try and get me but my gumbies are too big. My mum wears her gumbies when she watches me play footy so she can walk through the mud. My Dad would like to go to Sydney in his gumbies and meet you.

FROM:
NEIL (aged 8)

Banbeach
Victoria

For years two pairs of old black gumboots stood outside the back door. One day a small pair of yellow boots cuddled next to them. Since then the little yellow gumboots have grown and multiplied. I think there is something going on between those old black gumboots!

FROM:
J. TRUMAN
Woodside
South Australia

Gumboots

I loved it when the rain poured down
When I was just a kid,

FROM:
HELEN
BRUMBY
Rose Bay
Tasmania

And I didn't moan and groan and pout
Like other people did.
I'd put on my yellow raincoat -
Much the shade of butter,
Slip on my little black gumboots
And go wading in the gutter.
As I splashed on through the torrents
I hoped Mum wouldn't see;
She didn't know what fun it was -
She'd probably slap me!
But on went my little black gumboots
A-splashing and a-sploshing
With waves and waves of water
A-splishing and a-washing.
And my heart was full of happiness
Despite the cold and damp,
As I made my little black gumboots
Go tramp, splosh, tramp, splosh, tramp.

And now, when rain comes teeming
And streaming down the gutter,
I yearn for my little black gumboots,
And a coat the shade of butter.

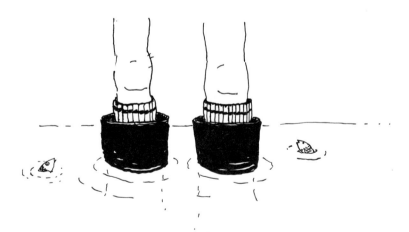

'SPLINTER'

Splinter the Swaggie just rang me up one morning. He phoned a few more times and sent me some letters, too, about his attitude to life. Splinter was a bit different to the rest of us: he just wandered around. He was a swaggie and, as his letters and phone call explained, he liked the lifestyle.

I think Splinter's calls and letters touched everyone who listened to the program. I was thinking about him one day and I remembered a poem by Robert Louis Stevenson I learnt in primary school. I think it sums up Splinter perfectly. It's called

The Vagabond

Give to me the life I love,
Let the lave go by me,
Give the jolly heaven above
And the byway nigh me.
Bed in the bush with stars to see,
Bread I dip in the river—
There's the life for a man like me,
There's the life for ever.

Let the blow fall soon or late,
Let what will be o'er me;
Give the face of earth around
And the road before me.
Wealth I seek not, hope nor love,
Nor a friend to know me;
All I seek, the heaven above
And the road below me.

'SPLINTER'

FROM:
NEVILLE
'SPLINTER' WOODS
Finley, NSW

I'm one of those coves who people like to think have long gone from Australia, a thing of the past . . . a swagman! I've been an avid listener of *Australia All Over* since Adam's grandfather got his H.S.C. I enjoy the singalong songs that you play but you are missing out on a good one called 'Billy of Tea' by the Bushwackers. It's on their album, The Bushwackers Collection and is very popular on the Darling Downs where I get to now and again. Give it a spin sometime if you can.

At present I'm camped at one of my favourite possies on a waterhole shaded by a clump of weeping willowtrees about three miles north of Finley. A good mate of mine, Max Wilson, a swaggy from the Great Depression Years, and his good wife Joan own a mobile general store in Finley and look after me well. They are fans of your show like me.

I'm 46 years of age now and have humped a swag around since the age of ten. I took off three hours after my father (Cranky Mick) turned up his toes. Like he always told me to do.

I'm the eldest of eleven kids and the only one in the family that is rurally inclined, the rest of the family being city dwellers.

I got the nickname Splinter from following my old man around the shearing sheds of Queensland where his shearer mates called him 'Timber'. When we'd lob up at a shed the old man's mates would say, 'Here comes Timber and the little Splinter with him.'

I come from a long line of swag humpers that go back to the 1890's. As well as being shown how to roll a swag by my father, other skills of survival have been passed down to me. I'm sorry that I don't have a son to pass on these skills to.

I've kept diaries of my life since I was fourteen years of age which someone may place value on one day.

I've been a prolific writer of bush yarns and verse and prose for years now but have trouble in publishing them. I keep running into people who try to con them off me because they take me as an empty-headed yokel simply because I hump a bluey.

I've been covered by numerous newspapers and have enclosed some copies of a few of them. I've also enclosed one of my stories so you can see the type of thing I write but don't let any mug try to publish it. It's for you only.

I'm presently working on getting a book published that is tentatively titled, 'Tales of a Swagman'. When I get it published I'll send you a copy.

I have to be constantly on my guard against people who want stories off me for their collection. I can't see any gain in my writing stories for somebody else to collect and make a quid out of.

I'm on an invalid pension now and am looking around for a property to live on in the Finley area so I can concentrate on the writing. These days, my knees are giving out and the ligaments in my feet ache like a politician's aspirations on election day.

The only regret I have about my travels is that I never got to meet Slim Dusty who I have great admiration for. I've lived several of his songs and would like to have met the bloke and shook his hand to say, 'Thanks mate, for the great songs'.

I've been meaning to give you a ring on a Sunday but I'm usually miles away from a phone then. I prefer to be out in the open air away from towns. I'll get round to it one day. If you acknowledge this letter on the air, don't do so till about 8 am as I don't usually fire on all pistons till about that time.

I know Bob Strickland from Parkes, the marbles championship bloke, having thrown my bluey in his truck and done a few miles with him. I haven't seen him for a while though, nor heard him speak on your programme, either.

I hope you like the photos, clippings, and the story. I've got in the habit of sending things like this to people to back up who I am as they tend to think blokes like me don't exist any more other than in magazine cartoons and jokes .

Keep up the good work with *Australia All Over*, for I believe it to be the only wireless show worth listening to for any great length of time.

I wouldn't be too concerned with the whingers who write in, for in my experiences I've come across people who only listen to the wireless and watch T.V. to find something to start a crusade about.

Give my mate Max Wilson and his wife Joan a call please Macca.

And don't forget that great singalong song 'Billy of Tea' by the Bushwackers. You'll love it.

Thanking you,

Splinter the Swagman.

As each day goes by it becomes more and more plain to me just how quickly this great country is losing its unique identity.

No more is this so painfully obvious than in the sad loss of character slowly being inflicted upon our railway system. This is particularly hurtful for me as a lot of my life has been hand in glove with the railways. I'm not merely referring to the practice of cadging rides on the trains but the overall destruction of a once loved tradition in this country— leisurely and friendly train travel with polite and caring staff in attendance.

I think a train is not a train without a guard's van on its ginger, and there are many around today that fall into this category. Years ago I shared many miles in the company of a guard who was glad of my company as well as others of my ilk. I forget the amount of times I've been camped at a siding only to have a train guard invite me aboard his train for a ride to wherever I wanted to go. When his shift finished I found his replacement to be equally polite and friendly. We always shared a billy or two of tea plus the odd lie or two as we outdid one another at spinning yarns to pass the time.

I recall standing by the side of a railway line on a hot day upending a bottle of beer as a train approached. When the steam engine got close, my mates and I would hold up a sugar bag full of bottles of beer packed in ice. The engine would soon stop and we'd get in with the driver and fireman, who'd be saturated in sweat from the heat of the engine's boiler. We'd take turns then in shovelling coal into the furnace to give the fireman a blow.

The greatest memories that I cherish about the railways are the stations. These were great meeting places for blokes on the track as they had large waiting rooms posssessed of long seats that made great possies to stretch out your tired frame for a camp. The station staff would always give you a 'hey' when they'd boiled the billy for a brew. I've sat out many big damps at a railway station's waiting room where I was treated as one of the family by stationmasters.

It both pains and angers me these days to find a grand old station has been demolished and replaced by a little dunny of a shed that a mouse would have trouble in doing a U-turn in. Two favourite station camps of mine were Grong Grong and Morundah (twenty miles south of Narrandera on the Newell Highway) but they've been pulled down and replaced by tin sheds. These two stations were extra good as camps for they had pubs right opposite them, which can only be classed as a bagman's paradise.

INTERVIEW with SPLINTER

'G'day, Macca, it's Splinter here. How're you going?'

Splinter the Swaggie! How are you?

'Oh, I'm having a rest, mate, from giving the flies and mozzies a free ride. Gotta get me strength back.'

I've read your letters with great interest, Splinter. How long have you been on the road?

'Since I was ten years old. A lot of people look at you real funny when you tell them that. They say, "How did you survive?" Well, I tell you what, you learn very quickly. You learn to keep the trusty old pickhandle handy.'

I bet! What keeps you on the road, Splinter?

'Well, you say to yourself, "Oh, I'll do this for a few years and then I'll give it up", but after a while you just can't. Like for instance, now I'm at Wangaratta. I only came here because it's a town I can walk out of in twenty minutes, put it that way.'

The nice thing, I guess, about life on the road is that you learn through the school of life and hard knocks; you learn lots of things about surviving and I suppose you also learn lots of trades.

'I think the main thing is that you learn how to be a human being. I have a lot of trouble at times. I live by the old Australian standards, you know, and I reckon they were pretty good for the older people and they're pretty good for me. I can go anywhere in this country because everywhere I go I leave an open door behind me. See, my old man taught me this. He said, "Now the rules are—stick to yourself, mind your own business, and take people as they come".'

And your Dad was called Cranky Mick?

'Yes, Cranky Mick. Ooh, he was a cranky bugger. Twenty-five stone he was, arms on him like a flaming gum tree.'

I hope I bump into you soon, Splinter, and have a yarn.

'I'd like to see you there one day but I think there's too many people camped in that city for me.'

There's too many people camped in Sydney, that's for sure. We'll talk again, Splinter. Good on you.

My name is David Williams, Wangaratta Police Station in Victoria. I was saddened to hear of the death of 'Splinter' our swaggie.

'Splinter' spent a long time in and around our area, a very law-abiding person, with great respect for the police, a job with great difficulties, in his opinion.

As Watch-hour Keeper for some eight years he was well-known to us, but never as a 'customer'.

Your program is aptly named. One Sunday I was listening in Wangaratta, the next Sunday travelling north from Marree to see Lake Eyre.

I have written a number of poems about my late brother, 'Splinter'. I have enclosed three poems. I'll leave it to you to pick out the best one as I am no expert. On my trip down to Wangarratta I was quite shocked at the weight of his swag. I honestly don't know how he carried it around. Staff at the Wodonga Hospital had to put it on a wheel chair to bring it out as it was too heavy for them to carry. Would you also thank everyone who has given 'Splinter' a lift in the past and helped him in any other way.

Last Farewell

'Splinter', the Swagman
Neville 'Splinter' Woods, was his name,
Thumbing lifts was his game.
A Swagman, true and blue;
The friendliest man, you ever knew.
Many a story he wrote, along the track,
Humping his swag, upon his back.
Here's to the brother, that we all knew,
And to the friends, that loved him too.

FROM:
V. G. LEISHMAN
Rockhampton
Queensland

'Splinter', the Rover

Described by himself as an inspector of roads,
Splinter travelled the compass points, not hurrying as he strode.
He'd seen things that many would not stop to see,
Many of nature's secrets he would see and the cost was free.
Weather-beaten by time, sun spots covered his tough skin,
A billy, a change of clothes in a swag, tied and rolled thin.
Many say his life was lonely, would they really know?
He had friends, God's creatures, no matter where he'd go.
He'd ring or write to Macca, this lonely travelling rover,
I know of quite a few who listened to his philosophy on *Australia All Over*.

'Splinter' was born in Rocky, the town where I now live,
Overcrowding and progress made him feel he had nought to give.
So with his swag and memories he headed for nature's rest,
Far away from the cities and the progress they possess.
There ought to be a lot more 'Splinters' roaming on this earth,
To show the flag of peace and harmony in the nation of their birth.
So farewell our friend 'Splinter', we know you are up above,
Looking down on the country that you know and love.
Your name is carved in many minds as 'Splinter' the Aussie Rover,
We'll hear your words of wisdom read by Macca on *Australia All Over*.

IN SOUTH AUSTRALIA

Performing 'Bundaberg Rum' with the
Overlanders in Adelaide.

At an Australia All Over concert in Renmark,
Ian danced the gumboot dance. His interview
with Joe Bredl caused some interest . . . Sally
Troy is holding another snake!

NEILREX, NSW
September 1990

In September 1990 the program was broadcast from Neilrex in New South Wales when there was a Back to Neilrex weekend and dance. Barry Rivett is with the outside broadcast van and Ian is talking to Cath.

3LO's Picnic in the Park

This was a great day at Melbourne's Myer Music Bowl in December 1990. Ian's interviews included one with Sister Sheila Mary. Later he appeared with the Gumboot band.

CHILDREN OUTBACK

David and Jacquie Ogilvy on the three-State post at Cameron's Corner. During his primary 'School of the Air' days, David used to ring Ian quite a lot. Then he went to high school in Broken Hill, where he visited Ian at 2NB.

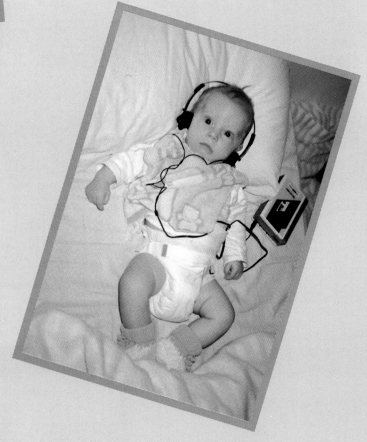

One of Australia All Over's youngest listeners, Robert Arvier, uses a Walkman to hear the Bird Symphony being broadcast.

TRAINS

The reason I talk about trains so much on the program is that people write about them. You only have to mention trains and people are writing about the demise of the train services; how old people can't get around on trains any more because now they're shunted onto buses on our inadequate road system; how their town used to be a centre for railways and how that town is now declining; or how their railway station, built in 1800 and something, is falling to bits because the line's closed and nobody cares.

It seems just about everybody in Australia has a railway story. I get more letters on *Australia All Over* about railways than any other subject, and these are just a few of them.

I like talking to railway people, especially stationmasters, guards and drivers, because they've travelled around the country and have seen lots of Australia. But it's getting pretty hard to talk to them now because there's not many of them left.

I still travel by train. I think luxury is travelling in a train in a sleeper; being able to sit up and have your tea or, in the old days, stopping at Albury Station and going off to the Refreshment Room to have a nice cup of tea or a pie or a toasted cheese and tomato sandwich.

Trains also encourage people to write romantic songs—how about this one!

There's this sheila in Refreshments
And she's serving cups of tea
And me heart jumps like a rabbit
When she pours a cup for me
She's got hair of flamin' yellow
Lips of flamin' red
And I'll love that flamin' sheila'
Till I'm up and gone and dead . . .

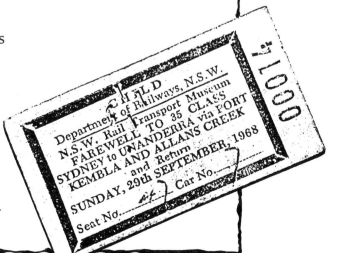

Sergeant Small was stationed at Quirindi and he used to dress up as a swagman to catch the swaggies who were riding the rattlers. He'd also dress up as a stockman and wander into camps looking for stolen stock. After I played a song about him on the program I got some letters and a phone call from his granddaughter, Joy Hines:

Good morning, Joy. How are you?

'I'm fine, thank you. My grandfather was a very wonderful person. I was about ten when he died.'

What do you remember about him?

'Well, he was big and had lovely curly hair. We lived with our grandparents for a little while and everyone would come and say, 'Where's the Sergeant?' We were very young and we just called him Sargy. We never called him Grandfather or Pop or anything like that.'

What did your parents say about him? Was he liked or was he feared? My grandfather was a policeman and he used to tell me about walking round country towns and kicking young troublemakers in the bum and things like that.

'He was never like that from what I can remember. I used to walk down the street with him sometimes and everyone used to say hello and be quite friendly. I don't think he was held in fear like the song makes out. He was round quite a lot of the country areas, stationed in Dubbo and Wee Waa and Nabiac.'

I know Tex Morton was on the wallaby at one time and so he may have bumped into Sergeant Small, but I don't know if Tex had a direct confrontation with him. I gather there was an injunction taken out by your parents or grandparents?

'No, by his brother, who was also a policeman. He was a Sergeant Small from Petersham. He took out the injunction to stop the record and I think all the records were recalled.'

Was it played on the radio at the time?

'Oh, yes. I'm pleased that I heard your program and that I was able to tell you that he wasn't the sort of person that this song made him out to be.'

from SERGEANT SMALL
by Tex Morton

Riding down from Queensland
On a dirty timber train
We stopped to take on water
In the early morning rain
I saw a hobo coming by
He didn't show much fear
He walked along the line of trucks
Saying 'Any room in here?'
Then I pulled the cover back and said
'Throw your blankets in'
He dropped his billy and his roll
And socked me on the chin
They took me to the jailhouse
And got me in a cell
I realised then who he was
It wasn't hard to tell
I wish that I was fourteen stone
And I was six feet tall
I'd take a special trip up north
And beat up Sergeant Small
I've worked with Jimmy Sharman and
At fighting I'm no dunce
But let me see the fellow
Who can take on five at once

I wish that I was fourteen stone
And I was six feet tall
I'd take a special trip up north
And beat up Sergeant Small.

As a very small lad of five I lived near the railway gates at Willow Tree and opened and shut them for the motorists queued up on both sides. Pennies and half-pennies were the usual payment for speeding the motorist on his way. But if only one car was there, and if it happened to be on the other side of the train, we crawled underneath the goods wagons. The goods train made scraping, scratching, screeching, creaking, banging, sliding, grinding noises as it slowly moved towards the shunting area. It was such a weird range of unrhythmical sounds running the full auditory scale that it always reminded me of the magpies' arpeggio.

What Sergeant Small thought about small boys acting as unofficial gate keepers (and soliciting alms in a public place!) could be judged by his frequent arrivals in his side-car.

As a matter of interest, to condition ourselves to the thought of being under a train at all, we crawled under the small culverts and lay on our backs looking up at the rattling monster above us. Hot sparks from the coal in the firebox sometimes dampened our enthusiasm!

I lived with my grandparents on the railway line. My granddad, Jumbo Evans, was the ganger and we lived in an old house between the trolley shed and the railway station. As kids we knew as much about trains as those who worked the line.

Sergeant Small never dressed as a swagman. Sure, he'd go along the train and round up a few, but he never dressed like them. He was *not* a cruel policeman. He was tough, but no one got hit or booted. My grandfather was a big man—six feet tall and eighteen to twenty stone, hence the name Jumbo. When Small wanted men picked up from the trains, which he had to do at regular times, he sent for Jumbo, but granddad let go more than he caught—he wasn't as tough-hearted as he was big.

When Tex Morton's song was released granddad laughed his head off and told us it was him, not Small, who knocked on the trucks and said 'Any room up there?' and Morton said, as most men did, 'Yes, throw your gear up'. Granddad said, 'You get yours out, and yourself, too!'.

However, our local six feet three or four constable, John Tanner, objected to the song. Years later Tex Morton brought his rodeo show to town and I went to it with my grandfather. Just as Tex announced to the crowded tent that he'd sing a song about our local policeman, into the entrance stepped our tall Constable John Tanner! He said, 'You sing that song and I'll pull the tent down'. Tex laughed and said, 'You and who else?' Tanner said, 'Me and that fellow over there', pointing to my grandfather. Tex turned and looked and that was enough—he recognised the big man all right. He pulled at his stetson and said, 'Well, we'll sing something else.' Tanner walked out of the tent.

FROM:
DAVID O'CONNOR
Wilson
Western Australia

Hearing you talk (again!) about railways reminded me of my arrival in Australia twenty-five years ago. I had hitchhiked from England and had arrived in Darwin with $2 left. How's that for exact budgeting, I thought, until I looked at the map to see how far it was to Sydney, my destination.

I got a job for a while in the bush out of Pine Creek on a railway maintenance gang, and then, pockets refreshed, hitched on. When I reached Julia Creek I was travelling with a man who was driving an MGB sports car. Twenty-five years ago that road was almost entirely unsealed and the MGB wasn't handling the trip too well, so he decided to put it on the train at Julia and not get off until he reached the bitumen at Pentland, about 400 kms away.

I was then still very much an Englishman and had never in real life seen railway carriages like these, but I recognised them from the Western movies I'd been hooked on at the Saturday morning flicks! They had the platforms at each end of the carriages and pull-down roller-blinds; they were old and hard-used and altogether wonderful! We bucked and rattled along at,—oh, I don't know, maybe five miles an hour—for what seemed like years; we were in a world of our own. We watched a dust-storm build up to blanket the sky as we eventually rode through it and came out the other end, each carrying our own supply of Queensland red soil.

When we reached Hughenden we sat immobile for half-an-hour until the guard came round to tell us that the engine had broken down. 'No worries,' he said, 'we'll soon fix her. Youse can all go down to the pub—we'll toot the whistle when she's ready to roll!' So we did. It took four hours to fix the engine so when the whistle blew it took a little time to climb up the steps into the carriages! We slept the rest of the way to Pentland, where the bitumen began, and rejoined the modern world with some regret.

I've been on many of the great trains of the world, including the CP through the Rockies and the Trans-Siberian across the steppes, but Julia Creek to Pentland via Hughenden holds a special place in my heart.

FROM:
RALPH PRESCOTT
Booragul, NSW

I can't believe anyone can be as enthusiastic about steam trains as you seem to be!

I used them before 1920 and found them filthy. I have been behind the 3801 in a two-hour and three-minute trip from Newcastle to Sydney and it rocked from side to side. At each of the tunnels (eight, I think) the windows would go bang, bang, bang but the carriages always filled with smoke. If anyone sat near the open window a cinder was almost certain to enter his or her eye.

My last twenty-eight working years were spent teaching at Cessnock High. The coal wagons were still being pulled by steam locomotives and it was uphill from Cessnock to the road crossing at Kearsley, where the brakes were pinned down for the downhill run to Neath.

Whenever a southerly was blowing our classrooms were filled with thick, evil-smelling smoke, so you may see why I don't agree with your enthusiasm for steam locomotives!

As a boy of about ten years I was living between Ganmain and Matong. We fronted the railway line and it was common practice for the swaggies to jump the rattler on the incline. They were numerous because dole was handed out at Narrandera, Grong Grong, Ganmain and Marrar and they had to move from one centre to the other each week. My mother's top tally for one day was twenty-one begging for food. She never refused anybody.

Once on board the train the swaggies would get under the tarpaulin. There was a railway policeman who would walk along the platform with a rubber hose and flog every bump he saw, especially if it moved. There was a well-known record then called 'Wingie the Railroad Cop', so named for the tramps he winged and arrested. Was that Sergeant Small?

Listening to stories of Tasmania, especially the west coast, reminded me of what I believe was the most interesting ride I have ever had in a 'motorcar'. In 1954 the father of a friend of mine was manager of the Emu Bay Railway Company which operated the railway from Burnie to Zeehan, Strachan and then to Queenstown. He suggested that as he was doing an inspection trip south I could travel with him in his 'car'. This surprised me, knowing there are no roads to Zeehan, but to my further surprise I saw a four-door Chevrolet, all nicely polished, sitting on the rail tracks. Its normal wheels had been replaced by train wheels! Perhaps the most interesting aspect of all was the fact that while it had a clutch, brakes, accelerator pedal, and manual gear change on the floor, it did *not* have a steering wheel, which I can assure you looked very odd. The driver did everything a driver normally does, except steer—

the tracks did that for him. It rained on the way down (as it usually does) and the wipers kept a clear vision for us.

The wonderful scenery and the remarkable cuttings through which we 'drove' were memorable and the entire trip by 'car' is one which I have never forgotten.

Here is a train story for you from Gippsland. In the days before motor cars were for everybody, the local football teams used to travel by train to the various venues between Bairnsdale, Maffra and Sale. Paddy Slavin was the driver and he had an ingenious method of spreading the match results on the return journey. As the train approached each hamlet or town he sounded the whistle, a long drawn-out howl for a loss and a series of 'cock-a-doodle-doos' for a win. If the match had been of some consequence, the home of the winning team got such a prolonged whistle that on more than one occasion the train ran out of steam and came to an unscheduled stop! And there it had to stay until sufficient steam could be raised to send it on its way. Many local people have vouched for the truth of this story.

Keep the trains rolling. It's the only way to go for us oldies. Leisurely. People to talk to, and time to make friends with, pampered at meals and comfortable sleeping compartments. Four days there on the train, hectic week in Sydney, and four days back on the train to unwind and savour the week in a strange land—Sydney.

Another reason I love train travel is because of the immediacy of departures and arrivals.

Before departure time friends and rellies can inspect the train from end to end: the sturdy diesels that are going to pull this long train from one side of Australia to the other; watch the luggage and the pets being loaded into the guard's van; count the vehicles on the double-decker transporter.

Kids specially love to get in the train and check out the bunks and the loos. Before you can stop them they have used and flushed the loos right there at the station. Kids! Everyone sits in the lounge and looks out at the other people on the station.

Time to go. Quickly make sure all the kids are accounted for; onto the platform to wave goodbye. Train starts. You can walk beside the train blowing kisses until the train gathers speed or you run out of platform.

Cards from anywhere along the Trans train line say it all. 'Having a good time'. Friends and family can imagine it all: the sound and rock-and-roll of the train, the dining room, the lounge and sleeping time.

On arrival, 'There they are!' excitedly as the train slows and stops. Hugs and kisses as soon as you step on to the platform.

It doesn't happen at airports or wharfs.

FROM:
DAVE COGGINS
Beachmere
Queensland

Last week a bloke rang you about the old railway to Alice Springs, and as I have just recently come back from a return trip on the New Ghan, I have some information about the old track and the Old Ghan.

The narrow gauge railway was completed to Oodnadatta in 1891, where it stopped for nearly forty years, earning the name of the 'Railway to Nowhere'. The first Ghan ran on 30th August, 1923 from Terowie to Oodnadatta, via Quorn. Terowie is just south of Peterborough (then called Petersburg) and was the junction of the narrow gauge (3'6″) and the broad gauge (5'3″) from Adelaide.

In 1929, the line finally reached Alice Springs, and the Ghan then ran from Quorn to Alice Springs fortnightly, leaving on Thursday afternoon and arriving on Saturday afternoon. The opening of the standard gauge track from Port Pirie to Port Augusta in 1937 diverted the east-west traffic via the coastal route, and the Ghan then travelled from Port Augusta.

During the war years the line carried saturation traffic, as supplies were carried north and injured brought south. The Ghan continued to provide an essential service and after the war it became very popular, on some occasions carrying six sleeping cars and two dining cars.

The Ghan was hauled by diesel locos for the first time in 1954, and by 1956 it had become so popular it was running twice weekly. The standard gauge track (4'8.1/2″) was completed to Maree in 1957, bypassing Quorn and the Pichi Richi Pass. The Ghan then ran from Maree to Alice Springs, with a connecting service from Port Augusta to Maree, and in 1961 air-conditioned carriages were introduced which made the Ghan more comfortable but less romantic.

The line from Maree to Alice Springs was subject to constant flooding in wet seasons and sand drifts in the dry, and approval was given in 1970 for a new standard gauge track to be built from Tarcoola to Alice Springs, bypassing the problem areas. This was completed in 1980, and the last Old Ghan ran on 26th November 1980. The first New Ghan ran on the new track on 4th December 1980, and the old track was pulled up between Maree and Ewaninga (about 30 km south of Alice Springs) from 1981 to 1983. Most of the old rail has gone to Queensland for use on the sugar mill tracks.

The remaining track from Macdonnell to Ewaninga is being used by the Ghan Preservation Society to run steam and diesel trains with some of the original rolling stock, and a visit to Macdonnell is essential for rail fans.

The present day Ghan is definitely the best train in Australia, and would be among the world's best—definitely worth a trip.

Here is a train story which I hope you'll enjoy.

Like you, my son is a train fan—or should I say fanatic?—and in his case signs of the addiction were evident from a very early age.

When my sister was married the ceremony was held at a small church near the local railway station. My husband and I, with three-year-old son, arrived at the church a little late, so slipped in to take a seat at the back, only to find that the bride herself was not yet there.

The bridegroom kept looking anxiously over his shoulder. The clergyman, with other weddings in mind, glanced repeatedly at his watch, and the guests were fidgeting and whispering together as they grew restive. Still the bride did not come, and the tension mounted.

Suddenly a shrill, excited voice was heard from the back of the church, 'Here she comes! Here she comes!'

The clergyman signalled to the organist, the congregation stood up in a body and turned towards the entrance door.

But what a dreadful anti-climax followed!

By climbing up behind the seat, son had managed to look out a window, and *she* was a train drawing into the station. The bridegroom wilted visibly, the guests sank down again in dismay, we were all so busy recovering from the disappointment that when eventually the bride did arrive, she was half way down the aisle before anyone noticed.

My son is grown up and married now himself. He and his bride spent much of their honeymoon touring by train. They are now rearing another generation of train-lovers on a diet of *Thomas the Tank Engine* stories, frequent steam train excursions, etc. Even the littlest one can recite magic numbers such as 4427 and 3801, which every good train buff should know.

Knowing your great affection for railways, I thought that you might like a brief account of an experience I had in early November, 1940, when I was nineteen. I was travelling by train from Melbourne to a new job with radio station 2QN Deniliquin. It was around mid-afternoon, very hot, and the train was rattling along at a fair bat on a long flat stretch between Echuca and Deniliquin. As many of the passengers had been travelling up from Melbourne since about 8.30 that morning they had given up reading their papers and were dozing the miles away. But all of a sudden there was an unexpected application of the brakes and the train ground to a halt. I put my head out of the open window, puzzled by the stop, as there was no station or siding for miles around, just the hot, flat plains of the southern Riverina baking in the shimmering heat. Watching the engine up ahead I noticed the driver and fireman alighting, so I presumed there was either some mechanical problem or that someone had pulled the communication cord because of an emergency. But no, they began walking away from the train towards a fence where they were joined by the guard, and the three of them then headed due west across a paddock to a farmhouse about two hundred yards away.

What did it all mean? Theories abounded among the deserted passengers. Was there a strike looming, was one of the crew too ill to go on, perhaps they needed to get to a phone? But there seemed to be no telephone wires to the house. So, totally mystified, we just sat perspiring in the sweltering carriages awaiting further developments— perhaps for ten minutes or so. Then, at around five minutes to three, we saw the trio returning talking animatedly among themselves and apparently exchanging money. Suddenly it dawned on us what they had been up to— they had been listening to the broadcast of the Melbourne Cup on the farmer's wireless. It was an unforgettable little episode. I have always felt that it gave an interesting insight into one small slice of life in rural Australia at that time. Where else in the world would a train stop for a horse race 200 miles away?

You were speaking about motor trains and I thought you may enjoy my experience with one. In the 1930s I was a relieving teacher in the north-east of Victoria and had to travel from Katamalite to Cobram. The mode of travel was a Buick car on the rails, painted black and yellow, with no steering wheel and above the driver's head was this sign which read:

IF CONVENIENCE
REQUIRED
ASK DRIVER
TO STOP

As you can imagine what the convenience was, one didn't ask the driver to stop!

I was a fourteen-year-old kid with three younger brothers when we lived in Bridgewater in the Adelaide Hills in 1936. Our property bordered the Melbourne-Adelaide line, and we never ceased to race to 'our' little wooden bridge to wave the engine drivers through, or down to the cutting to see the trains heave up the grade. It was a slow haul in frosty weather

with ice on the rails. The engine would keep slipping back, even though they poured sand from a pipe near the wheels to help them grip the rail. I've known them to be stuck there for at least half an hour, slipping back, wheels spinning aimlessly, and on winter nights their bright headlights would shine through the kitchen window where I was washing up—a great boost to our kerosene lamps.

Of course in those days it was the good old steam train—no air conditioning.. With open windows you'd sometimes get soot blowing in, and lovely clouds of white and grey smoke billowing from the chimneys. The chugging of the engine and the clickety-clack as they rode over the rails were music to our ears.

On Sundays we'd go down to the cutting to watch the Melbourne express charge through. We used to call out 'paper' and from the long line of windows people would throw out their papers and magazines— The *Herald*, *Truth* and similar papers, and sometimes a *Man* magazine— a very saucy one in those days. Mum and Dad would confiscate them, and we'd end up with the comics, but we were happy with that.

One morning, as we called out, a lady held up a box at the window of the train, pointed at it, then tossed it. We raced down after it and discovered at least a dozen beautifully iced and decorated small cakes— none the worse for their flight and heavy landing.

We used to walk for miles along the line, picking wildflowers on the way. When we'd get to a deep cutting, we'd put our ear to the rail to make sure a train wasn't coming before we ventured into the long cutting with only a foot track on either side of the line. We were always careful before going into a tunnel, though one day we only just made it out when an unusually fast train came through.

Another interesting sight for us kids was the railway cars running along the line at intervals, with grooves on the wheels instead of tyres, and the man-hauled scooters that the fettlers rode to check the rails and sleepers. Alongside the cutting were lots of blackberry bushes, and in season we'd pick buckets of beautiful luscious berries. After we'd stuffed ourselves there'd still be enough for Mum to make blackberry pies, and tarts and jam!! They were luscious served with thick cream separated from the milk of our two cows.

In recent years I went back to Bridgewater and walked the old tracks. There, where 'our' little bridge still stands, are the enormous freeway bridges overpassing the solid little one we always used. These new bridges cut right through our old property, but in the distance you can still see the pine trees Mum planted all those years ago.

Our neat little railway station was gone as well, burnt out in horrific bushfires some years back. It was never replaced. I stood there on the platform, looking round; so desolate now—but they can't erase my memories of yesteryear. I can still see and hear the whistle of the train as the engine driver answered our waves from the little wooden bridge. I can still hear the heave and strain of the big goods trains trying to get through our cutting.

I now travel in style and comfort on the Indian Pacific or Trans Australian when I visit my two sons and families in South Australia. It's a far cry from the good old days, but in my old age I need the comfort.

I was struck by the song about Sergeant Small. I wonder if there was another Sergeant Small in Queensland. There is a poem, 'Battling Days', by Wilfred Frost, which I put into the *Penguin Book of Australian Humorous Verse* which credits Sergeant Small with a Queensland hunting ground. The specific verse reads:

Hard we battled and often we lost
Battling over the blacksoil plain
By Sergeant Small, how we were tossed
From the trucks of a Queensland train.

FROM:
BILL SCOTT
Warwick
Queensland

I remember the raids on the trains at Caboolture when I was a boy. Because we were the first dole town north of Brisbane many blokes jumped the rattler there to pick up their dole, and quite often the police would raid the trucks. It was like putting a ferret down a rabbit hole— blokes scattering into the wallum followed by sprinting constables. Our house was near the railway goods yards so we kids had a grandstand view from our front verandah. Naturally, our sympathies lay with the hoboes.

But there were many sympathetic policemen who gave the hoboes a fair deal so long as they played the game and didn't make trouble. The police had an instruction to keep them moving and they certainly tried to do that, but not all of them were tough on the swaggies. Most of them would help a man get work if they heard about a job going and closed their eyes to a man down on his luck.

After hearing about the Croydon-Normanton rail motor I could not contain myself. What a wonderful description the lady from Mayvale Station gave. My grandparents were on Mayvale for fifty years and my parents were married there by a Church of England bush brother. My parents took my brother and I up there for a holiday when I was seven and he eight years old. It took us a week to get there from Cairns. At each creek or river women and children were taken across in a steel boat and the men carried the luggage and waded across with it over

FROM:
BERYL MICHAEL
Henty
NSW

their heads. Mother had packed fruit and food they seldom saw up there, and dear Dad's face revealed he wished she had only brought half!

What excitement when we arrived: it was all so worthwhile. We had a lovely week when the rail motor arrived—the event of the week! We all went down to Blackbull railway siding, the mail was collected and hot drinks and news given.

My brother really enjoyed watching the men with the droving, but wept when the calves had to be marked with a branding iron. I recall grandad proudly pointing out how he hand cut every sleeper on the railway line and the government paid him sixpence a sleeper. It gave me a proud moment when I heard the lady from Mayvale say the original sleepers were still in use.

In pre-World War II years we lived at Mt Isa, where my school-teacher father was sent to open the first secondary school in 1937. When school vacation began in December we headed off for holidays in Brisbane by the only means of transport—Queensland Railways.

The weekly passenger train out of Mt Isa departed on Monday mornings but, being eager to get away, we always left on the lead train on the afternoon of the Friday that school finished. The daily lead train to Townsville consisted of fifty or more open wagons loaded with lead ingots and a seats-only coach-cum-guard's van at the rear.

Our train dragged laboriously eastwards across the plain all through Friday night, throughout the entire Saturday and the next night, arriving at Townsville on Sunday around breakfast time. There we waited all day to connect with the Brisbane Mail on Sunday night, eventually pulling into Brisbane on Tuesday.

The long haul on the lead train must have been a nightmare for my parents. No sleepers, no dining car; toilet and food stops whenever we passed through isolated places such as Cloncurry, Hughenden and Julia Creek, and clouds of soot from the straining loco pouring through the windows, which had to be left open in the hot December weather. Worse still was the incessant noise. At every upgrade the loco forged ahead and each wagon in succession dropped back on the couplings with a jerk and a clang, a jerk and a clang, a jerk and a clang, right back to the coach. Having breasted the rise we then coasted down the incline, the whole train closing up in concertina fashion, all the wagons gaining momentum and in turn crashing noisily on to the buffers of the wagon ahead, crash, jerk, crash, jerk— all over again.

We kids always enjoyed the adventure of these journeys, gazing out the window with eyes screwed up to keep out the soot, intrigued by the wide brown land, the shimmering mirages on the vast horizon, and the occasional flocks of emu and brolga—all the time lulled by the repetitious click-clack of the wheels and the creaking of the old timber coach frame.

However, for parents it must have been a helluva trip, trying to provide and carry adequate food, babies' bottles, bedding and all such necessities for a family. Oh for the good old days!

FROM:
Br. David O'Brien
Glenorchy
Tasmania

My name is Brother David O'Brien and I belong to an order in the Catholic Church called the Salesians (Sal-ez-yuns) who look after youth in schools, youth clubs, hostels, boys' towns, parishes and holiday camps.

Prior to joining the order I worked as an engineman on the Victorian Railways. I didn't get my Driver's Ticket, but I worked my way to Engineman Class 2 (Drivers are Class 3). In the old language I would be called a Fireman.

In the years before I joined the railways I wouldn't have cared two hoots (pardon the pun) for trains. Even as a kid my interest was more in cars, but I believe that when you are involved in railways it somehow gets into your blood.

I enjoy reading about railways—both historic and modern. I also enjoy listening to stories, and, even better, telling stories of the railways. Like the times we used to run trains to Hamilton from Warrnambool in south-west Victoria in the late '70s. I only worked on DEs—i.e. diesel electrics; they're not steam, but they have an aura about them just the same. We used to leave Warrnambool at around ten in the morning with about ten trucks and a van.

Now the line between Koroit and Hamilton was in a bad state and had a speed limit of ten mph. Also, the track was as flat as a billiard table and there weren't many level crossings. They were perfect conditions for some strange and funny goings on—the driver going rabbit shooting while the guard and fireman played cards in the guard van; or all three going mushroom picking while the train went merrily on its way. Many a good book could be read cover-to-cover on this trip while the 'Y' class with the ten trucks rattled very slowly on.

On the way home, we would sometimes cook our produce, especially the mushrooms. This is what I would say is the adventure of the railways— a bit of fun, a bit of getting away with it, and a bit of getting the job done in the most pleasant manner possible.

FROM:
JOAN FORD
Cowra
NSW

Before long there will be no older generation to reminisce about the days of travelling by steam. No stories of waiting in lonely, cold, windswept stations at midnight huddled in front of blazing log fire for the connecting train to take one back to boarding school after the Easter break. No stories of the last hurried goodbyes or last instructions exchanged between parents and children as the train came noisily into view. 'Here are your sandwiches and a piece of a cake . . . don't eat it all at once . . . wash the apple first . . . where's your hat? . . . have you got your ticket? . . . don't speak to strangers on the train . . . be good . . . remember to write every week!' Anxious little faces pressed against the window, brave smiles as Mum appears to get smaller and smaller as the train draws away from the station.

I recall my father proudly telling us that he played in the local brass band on the Glen Innes Railway station every time a train came through the town from Queensland carrying troops or enlisting men down to Liverpool, Sydney, during the First World War. They played every man in the district away on the train going to war. He said the band consisted of old men and young boys in those days; all the other band members had gone to the Front. His father, William Coughlan, was the Bandmaster and he and his brothers were members of this band. At all hours of the night they would be wakened up to go down to the station. Lighting their way with a kerosene lamp carried on a pole and lit with a wick, they would arrive at the station to play old songs like 'It's a Long Way to Tipperary', 'Bless 'em All', 'Pack Up Your Troubles', 'It's A Long Long Trail a-Winding', as the train came through Glen Innes.

The Dirranbandi Mail Train is the last to run on a regular basis with wooden sleeping car accommodation. It is also a freight train and shunts off louvre wagons at each major town on its slow journey to Dirranbandi. It picks up wagons on its return journey.

Country people, especially west of Goondiwindi, still come to meet the Mail to pick up parcels, meat and newspapers, something that is now only a memory in other states.

A reporter writing a travel article for the *Sydney Morning Herald* said that the Dirranbandi Mail was Queensland's best-kept secret. If you are looking for something different to do on your holidays try a return trip from Brisbane on the Dirranbandi Mail. Take a large thermos and some edibles though!

CRICKET

If you haven't been listening to *Australia All Over* for long you probably won't understand the significance of the 'I Made a Hundred' saga. It started in 1987 when my Mum heard the song somewhere and told me about it, so I played it a couple of times. Then Russ King, a mate of mine who works for the ABC in Mackay, sent down a story to *Australia All Over*. On the front of the story he said, 'Listen, Macca, if you play that song again I'll crack up. Cut it out!' So of course I played it again and invited people to sing along. It was a good song and most people liked it.

As a young boy I loved cricket—backyard, frontyard, anywhere—and there's usually a cricket story every other week.

'I made 100' float from Yarram State School, Victoria

CRICKET

Thanks for getting me through defrosting the fridge. While I'm listening to your program I'm not in my kitchen at all. I'm encountering Stone Age Aborigines in the desert, flying with a pilot in a jet over the Nullarbor, being cosy in a hut in the ice and snow of Antartica, or sharing a cuppa with the friendly staff of a railway station somewhere out Woop-Woop! This morning's finale, though, made me laugh out loud (I'm here by myself)! I could just imagine Australians all over, turning up their radios and singing full belt 'I Made a Hundred in the Backyard at Mum's' to the amazement and amusement of any ETs flying over our continent at the time!

In Kenmore, signs read 'Danger, cricket balls in vicinity, be careful'. Yes, you heard—my 15-year-old next door neighbour and me have come a 'traffic hazard'.

Every Saturday afternoon around 2.30pm (daylight saving time) it's crash! bang! ouch! howzat! Another day, another sixty-four dints in the old metal bin.
Our statistics read: Hit windows—seven (me four times, Michael three)
Broken windows—one (me)
Broken fingers (in gate)—two (me)
Smashed stumps—eight
Broken bat handles—one

Every Sunday morning at about 10.15 (after *Australia All Over*) it's snick, bang, howzaaat! 'Here we go again!' cry our mothers and fathers. The rules are:
1 Over the fence on the full (backwards and forwards) is out.
2 Bowled is out.
3 Can't get out first ball.
4 Hit the aviary on the full is out, plus dead birds, guinea pigs and rabbits.
5 On the road rolling is four and out.
6 Caught and bowled is out.
7 Hit in the head is out cold.
8 If your bat nicks the ball and hits the back wooden fence you're caught behind.

We started off playing with a tennis ball in Michael's yard but we hit too many windows by hooking the ball. Then we played with a tennis ball on the road but we lost hundreds. Next we played in the backyard with a tennis ball but we kept losing them. We didn't want to move again so we covered the tennis ball with tape. Failed—a dog from down the street thought it was a meatball and started eating it. So now we use a cricket ball and so far only one has been lost.

I play for my school every Friday and so far my highest score has been four off two balls faced. My worst was against Indooroopilly when I was bowled second ball for a duck. I think the best backyard game I played was in Mt Isa with my cousin Brian, my uncle David, my Mum and Dad. Dad was naughty. First he hit my Aunty-in-law's car, leaving a little dint, and then he hit the next picnic lot with a cut shot. He knocked a plate of lamb cuts from a woman's hand.

P.S. Beware of falling cricket balls.

You recently talked about your bush cricket innings and the ball which claimed your wicket probably hitting a rock on the pitch.

It reminded me of a story I heard as a member of HM's Colonial Service of cricket during the days of Empire.

Years ago, a visiting Royal Navy Fleet used to play an annual cricket match against one of HM's island colonies. The game, keenly contested by the islanders, was played on coconut matting laid on an earthen foundation. Traditionally, the Navy batted first to avoid fielding in the heat of the day. The penalty for this privilege, however, was batting unpredictably and dangerously during the morning session of play—until lunchtime, in fact.

What the sailors did not know, though, was that the conventional invitation to them to take first knock had a much higher purpose than a seemingly altruistic courtesy. It was, in truth, a device to ensure the islanders' fast bowlers took full advantage of the fiery pitch which had been liberally larded with bottletops hidden underneath the coconut matting!

The damage to the visitors' score, bodies and egos having been done in the first two hours of play, the coconut matting was rolled up and the bottle tops removed during the break for lunch, when the players were absent from the ground at the mayor's winery down the road. What remained of the Navy's innings and, of course, the whole of the local team's, was then played on a placid pitch. The unsuspecting sailors, bless 'em, always blamed the climate for the early erratic behaviour of the pitch.

This skulduggery continued for some years until the game in which the incumbent Navy team captain, a man with more than a touch of the professional in him, decided he wanted his team to bat second and so declined the customary offer from the opposing skipper.

Here was a switch! The islanders were to bat first! On their already doctored pitch! But were they fazed? Not a bit of it! The whole team, under the command of their captain, and in full view of their incredulous

FROM:
IAN D. St G LINDSAY
Kewarra Beach
Queensland

opponents, trooped out to the wicket, rolled up the mat, picked up the bottle tops and then relaid the mat!

You might be interested in this cricketing story.

Quite some years ago in Ouyen, in the Victorian Mallee, the local barber used to be the SP bookie on the side. One very hot February afternoon the Gaming Squad Police came down from Mildura and created a terrible panic.

The barber ran out of his shop, over the street, through the fence across the railway lines, through the other fence, over the highway, under the fence, into the sports ground and up the hill to the cricket oval. By this time he had just about had it. But he staggered onto the field, pushed the umpire out of the way, and stood there, gasping for breath. Just then the wicket keeper appealed, 'Howzat?', and the barber said, 'Not guilty'!

The Ultimate in Male Chauvinism
In the early 1930s Christchurch Cinemas, a picture theatre group in Christchurch, New Zealand, formed a cricket club and built a small, picturesque oval on the outskirts of that city.

A log cabin performed the role of clubhouse and, though the boundary fences were much smaller than the regulation fields, it nevertheless provided enjoyable cricket.

There was, however, an ironclad rule that no female should ever set foot on this hallowed ground with the exception of one day per year when a mixed picnic day was allowed! In view of this rigid rule the area was named—would you believe—the Valley of Peace!!

On your program on Sunday 7th September, you voiced a view that perhaps the game of cricket was declining in the country areas of Australia.

Times have changed and cricket has to compete with many other sports. Most country towns have tennis and squash courts, swimming pools, water-skiing, gun clubs, golf clubs, indoor cricket, etc. Also, roads have improved along with modern cars, and the lure of the big smoke or the beaches appear more attractive to the younger folk than hours on a cricket field.

There are many country areas still strong in cricket. Once football is finished and Border and his boys get busy again, you will find boys from six to sixty lining up on Saturdays dressed in white, with all the accessories ready to make a hundred or take ten wickets.

Chinchilla, two hundred miles west of Brisbane in Queensland, is one of the areas were cricket is keenly played. Here we could have many future Bradmans or Dennis Lillees, as the boys are very keen and have their heroes to emulate. Cricket has been played in the Chinchilla area since 1911 and the Chinchilla and District Cricket Association celebrated its 25th anniversary in 1990.

My Mum and Dad took me and my little sister for a BBQ yesterday at Kalimna Park at South Evans Head close to where we live.

While we were cooking our sausages and steak a big goanna about one metre long came out of the bush and looked at us.

Mum and my sister Kirryn screamed and jumped up on the picnic table but soon Dad and I had him tamed by feeding him cut up bits of sausage.

He hung around for a while and we decided to play a game of cricket.

We used the blackbutt tree as the stumps and I bowled one and dad hit it.

My brand new six stitcher landed near the goanna and he marched over and picked it up in his mouth and took off into the scrub with it.

We searched all over to find the goanna who knocked off the ball which stopped the match but couldn't find him.

So if anyone is at Kalimna Park and sees a goanna walking around with my cricket ball in his mouth can they please contact me because I would really like it back.

Dad said to me if the goanna had come back with the ball he would have put him on his team.

I am a semi-retired secondary school deputy principal who was fortunate to be raised in a cricket culture. Whilst worried about the decline in the numbers playing the game I would like to offer some suggestions for your program along the lines of 'This is where I have played and/or enjoyed cricket'.

I remember as a very young teacher playing cricket in the Phrennes Association in Central Victoria against the local prison team Langi Kal Kal. Here the players wore coloured clothing years before Kerry Packer introduced the idea and player dissent was at a minimum as the umpiring was done by two warders who were armed with rifles.

Recently I have had the opportunity to travel and have seen a great variety of cricket grounds. Scenically I think one of the nicest grounds is the one at Port Arthur in Tasmania. The ground at Tibooburra in

far northwestern NSW with its rock strewn oval would make most fieldsmen apprehensive. The only sight of green is a strip of artificial turf acting as the wicket. The Birdsville ground is at least in sight of the pub!

I write about the seagulls, those faithful fans who never miss a match. These brave birds will fly anywhere to see a game of cricket. And what they enjoy most are the international Test matches—they come in flocks. I don't know how far they travel each season to make sure they don't miss an over.

Surely they must be in training all through winter with special diets in order to have the stamina to stand in the outfield for hours and hours after flapping their way across kilometers of the countryside from one city to another. Do you think they use muscle-building drugs? True, I have never seen headlines such as:

STEROID TEST POSITIVE

SEAGULLS DISQUALIFIED FROM THE OUTFIELD.

But has an effective test been devised for seagulls?

I will give them one thing though, they are impartial. They don't show favour for any team nor take note of the scores. It's the game, the tradition of fair play that intrigues them. They see themselves as guardians to ensure that every move is cricket. Think of the agony they must have suffered when someone resorted to bowling an under-arm to safeguard victory a few years ago!

These dignified birds remain imperturbable, indefatigable and, what is more, impervious to remarks from the commentator's box. In fact, they sustain their superiority by being heedless of the opinions of mere humans. All the generations of breeding that have gone into learning to hover above the sea looking for food or trudging along empty beaches searching for left-over titbits have given them infinite patience. They do not get restless between overs when dozens of fieldsmen move around to find somewhere more comfortable, more out-of-the-way, any place where it is easier to drop a ball or not catch it at all. The seagulls treat these petty tactics with the disdain they deserve.

Also the gulls are fearless, even poor Jonathon's experience didn't deter them. I thought that it was the end for poor Jonathon when the ball hit him—an innocent bystander. He was a pitiful sight. There he was supine and still. However, like the great bird he is he rolled over, struggled to stand up, but toppled down again. Most undignified it was. Then a deep sigh of relief went through the stands as he rose up again.

I think he must have decided about that time that he'd had enough for one day. After all, while it may be considered Playing the Game

to hit one of the opposition on the field, it really is NOT cricket to strike the staunch supporters, the seagulls.

FROM:
DOROTHY MURPHY
Toowoomba
Queensland

I thoroughly enjoyed the letter from the lady in Toowong on the seagulls that frequent the cricket grounds around Aussie. It was beautifully written!

May I present a different viewpoint on what comes into my mind when watching these beautiful birds on the TV.

I imagine them being reincarnated cricketers. If you watch, they appear to talk to one another.

'You know,' says one, 'I used to be the wicketkeeper here.'

'Yes!' says another, 'I used to be batsman. And see those two over there on their own—they used to be the umpires. One comes from out back somewhere—Bullamakanka or Bandywallop.

One seagull nearby says, 'If you are here to watch the cricket, stop talking—you just missed A.B. hit a four.'

Some of them just squat down on their chest with feathers out, reclining in comfort.

FROM:
VICKI BRAGG
6B, OAK FLATS
PUBLIC SCHOOL
NSW

I Was A Fielder in the Backyard At Mum's

I was a fielder in the backyard at Mum's
I cut off a ball that was meant to be four runs
I dropped a chance first innings and the spectators looked glum
I was a fielder in the backyard at Mum's.

I tell you, it was dangerous around the yard that day
The way me brother batted put Viv Richards to shame
Sometimes it got so vicious that we had to duck and weave
And the old shed door couldn't take it, so we hid behind a tree.

Then me Uncle Nev came on to show us all the way
But me brother faced his fast balls and smashed them all away.
Me Grandma, although eighty, dived before one hit her head
And I think she got angry 'cause her grey hair turned to red.

I had a go at bowling and me offbreaks were superb
Me brother couldn't hit them and he said I was a nerd
But when our little brother bowled and caught him on the pad
Grandma raised her finger and the fielders all went mad.

Me brother scored a hundred and the neighbours yelled and cheered
But the fielders were rewarded as they downed a few more beers
The old shed door's replaced now and we're ready for more fun
I was a fielder in the backyard at Mum's.

WHY I LIVE WHERE I LIVE

The first 'Why I Live Where I Live' was from a bloke called Gil Wahlquist, who lives in Mudgee in New South Wales — that was back in February, I think, of 1986. He started like this:

> I'm speaking to you from Botobolar Vineyard at Mudgee. It's up in the Great Dividing Range. It's 2000 feet above sea level, and as I look out my window I can see the sun rising over the top of the range. Actually the water that falls on the top of the range, just where I can see it, sixteen kilometres away, finds its way down the Macquarie river to the Murray, and ends up in South Australia. And I suppose that always gives me a certain, well, warm feeling, because I grew up in South Australia and that's really what I regard as my home, if anyone asked me what my home was.

'Why I Live Where I Live' is without doubt my favourite part of the program because there are so many good letters. I decided when I started the segment that it would mainly be a correspondence thing, although sometimes I've talked to people. For instance, when I was in Griffith I talked to a bloke who said he lived where he lived because it was flat—'as flat as your hand, that's the one-tree plain'!

But most people write in. Sometimes they write sad stories about being deserted, or forced to live somewhere. Someone once told me that the letters are too good to be true because there are rarely any complaints. But most people are proud of where they live: I mean, why else would they live there? You wouldn't write and say 'I live in a rotten place' and publicise the fact Australia-wide!

'Why I live Where I Live' is a particular view each week of various aspects of Australian life.

FROM:
BOB MOON
Townsville
Queensland

This is a variation on 'Why I Live Where I Live'—'Why I'm Glad I Grew Up Where I Did'!

There might not appear to be anything special about growing up during the 1930s and 1940s in Waverley, a suburb of Sydney. What is important for me is that I grew up about 100 yards from Waverley Cemetery— only fifty yards if you were prepared to climb the fence, as we generally were.

I think we learned a lot about Australian history and tradition in an interesting and eccentric sort of way at the cemetery—or the cemo, as we knew it. There we looked at the grave of Roderic Quinn (I hadn't been aware that he lived in nearby Paddington until I heard your program), had snippets from 'The Camp Within the West' recited to us and went home to read more. The impressive grave of Henry Kendall is also there in a prominent corner position not far from one of the side gates of the cemo. And in a typically unadorned grave in an obscure position is Henry Lawson's.

But it wasn't just the poets we met at the cemo. We also admired 'the governor's grave'—I forget which governor it was—a big impressive plot guarded by metal lions and a chain fence. We learnt something of governors and parliaments and the fact that even the great are mortal.

Mortality was a central theme in two other parts of 'our cemo' that we came to know. At the gates there was a soldiers' memorial and the gates themselves were memorial gates. Each year a ceremony was held to celebrate the fallen of the Great War, in particular the Australians lost in France. The other great monument, in fact the biggest in the cemetery, is the Irish memorial to all the Irish patriots who died, especially in the Easter uprising of 1916. We were intrigued by the list of heroes named along the back of the monument—not that they were described as heroes to us, as kids. Our family, being English and Welsh by background and protestant by tradition, wasn't very enthusiastic about Irish Catholics. On Easter day when the great memorial service was held each year, we'd listen to the Irish pipers and hear the priests addressing the loyal followers. For us they certainly were not loyal and in the early 1940s, with Prime Minister Winston Churchill leading an embattled England, we were told of these terrible priests speaking against 'our own Mr Churchill'. Even if the history we learnt was biased, at least we became aware that the story was not a bland one but one of struggle and of conflicts of beliefs.

There is one other important aspect of Australian culture I first encountered at the cemo. The cemetery ends at a great cliff which drops a couple of hundred feet down to the sea. Just beside the cemetery and tucked into these cliffs was a huge cavern. On Sunday mornings we'd see men of all ages and types, singly and in twos and threes, drifting down to the cliff top and then picking their way along the narrow cliff face track to the cavern. Not all of them actually went down the track and into the cave; there were always five or six scattered around, standing idly, yarning and smoking. If we walked around the cliff a hundred yards or so the curve of the cliff allowed us to look back into the cave and observe a strange ritual. We could see the men standing in a great circle and then, as if at a signal, all the heads would go up and then down, looking to the floor, and there'd be a muffled roar that echoed from the cave. This went on time after time. I must say that since then I've seen two-up played at some of the ritzy casinos around Australia and they have nothing of the mateship, intensity and authenticity of the game as it was played in that sandy-floored cavern on bright Sunday mornings with the sea surging over the shelving rocks below.

There was excitement for us, too—one morning, a police raid. The cockatoos did the best they could to warn the gamesters but the cave was really a huge trap. Once the police reached the top of the cliff there were only two choices—walk up into the hands of the police or scramble on down the rough track and take to the water. And that's what some of the braver gamblers did. Luckily it was a calm day but, even so, once in the water it was almost impossible to get back onto the rocks, and the nearest beach, Bronte, was a very long way off even for good swimmers. So we watched the scuffling of police and players at the top of the cliff, others scrambling down the cliff and along the rocks below and other heads bobbing up and down wondering what to do next. This is Australia, so it wasn't the Mounties or the cavalry to the rescue but the lifesavers. In those traditional heavy wooden surfboats they rounded the headland and began to pick up the swimmers one by one. If I remember correctly, no-one was drowned, no-one was fined too heavily, and they all lived to play another day.

Where else but at Waverly Cemo could a kid get such an introduction to Australia?

Byaduk . . . I lived where I lived and loved it, because I was born there. Byaduk, meaning 'running water', derived that name from one of the Aboriginal tribes, the Buandik Tribe, who roamed areas from the Grampians. My Dad, full of tricks, said the name evolved from an Afghan wagoner who sold curries, spices and penny-royal. This merchant caught some ducks, then put a notice on his wagon, 'By-a-duk'.

It is a picturesque tiny village in a green volcanic valley formed by the extinct volcano Mount Napier. Population no more than one hundred within five miles of Jack's Store, where his delightful daughter sometimes pulls the petrol. Wow! The store-keeper is always good for a cheerful yarn. You can get ANYTHING from cornflakes, rakes, straw and wheat, to lollies to eat. There isn't a pub, coffee shop or disco. The blue-stone school has closed, and the butter factory. The stones from the demolished flour mill now form a fine porch at Macarthur's St. Malachi's Catholic Church.

Leaving his original Henry Berry oven many years ago, the fine old baker has gone to the blue yonder, also the village music teacher.

During the week tourists may think the place as dead as Whim Creek, but at weekends scores gravitate there to fight Byaduk for the A-Grade Cricket Championship on the turf wicket, or footy.

There's a fine stone church, originally Methodist, for spiritual refuelling on one Sunday each month. It is a paradise of beauty for a painter and peaceful joy for a writer. In two spots near my home spring waters drip from sandstone rocks. At North Byaduk there are three caves that few visit; only wild life and bats live there. But Americans have visited. My daughter, when sorting specimens for a palaentologist at Purdue, Indiana, found items from caves near Hamilton, Victoria, Australia. Interesting, wasn't it?

FROM:
DOROTHY PLAK
Woodville Gardens
South Australia

Poem written for the 150th Jubilee Year

South Australia has been good to me—
Under its wide blue sky I have found freedom;
In its golden hills I have known contentment;
In each dawn and sunset the peace that passeth understanding.

So much I will remember
When the time comes for my spirit to pass
Into the endless Dreamtime -
The wildflowers a blaze of colour
In the desert after rain;
The rich red earth of the Outback
Reflected in the galahs' wings at dusk;
The shades of Burke and Wills
In the camp beside the Darling;
And the dark people, telling me of their love
For this mighty land, to which, I also,
Give my love and gratitude, in return
For all that it has given me.

FROM:
WENDY GREEN
Kedron
Queensland

I live at Kedron, an inner northern suburb of Brisbane. Earlier this month I was holidaying with friends in Thailand. During our stay in Bangkok we met up with two Australian friends of ours, Denley and Leon, who have been living in Bangkok for the last five years. One evening we were travelling by taxi across Bangkok to have dinner at Leon's home. The traffic was absolutely horrendous, as it always is in Bangkok. We had been stationary in the traffic for at least twenty minutes and Denley, who lives in a unit in the heart of Bangkok, was telling us that it takes Leon two hours to get to work from his lovely traditional Thai house on the river. Denley then went on to explain that although he only has a very small high-rise flat in central Bangkok, it only takes him fifteen minutes to get to work. He then said 'And that's why I live where I live'.

Well Peter, Charmaine and I, who are all avid listeners of 'Australia All Over', immediately burst into song with 'And That's Why I Live Where I Live'. Denley looked at us as if we had all gone round the twist. We then explained the situation and are now taping the program to send to him so that he can hear the segment 'And That's Why I Live Where I Live' for himself.

I live in Candelo, a small village equidistant between Bega and Merimbula. I came to south eastern NSW from Melbourne some ten years ago and we set up a medical practice. My husband was a GP who was disillusioned with the pace of life in the city, and who wanted to get back to what he was really good at, family medicine. Candelo had not had a doctor for many years; and needless to say we were made very welcome. We were really enjoying rural life when my husband died, very suddenly, fifteen months after we came here.

At the insistence of my children we stayed on, although my initial feeling was to try to go back to Melbourne where we had friends and relatives, and I am glad that we did. The children enjoyed their country education despite the disadvantages of living a long way from a city. I think that the advantages far outweighed the disadvantages—growing up in a small, caring and safe environment, the beauty all around, the simpler joys of life—these things are priceless. The cultural things which they may have missed out on can be enjoyed later and probably with greater appreciation.

You often comment on the apathy of Australians to their environment and social problems, and I agree with your sentiments. It is sad how many of us don't value what we have (or had) and are not prepared to speak up and act to prevent further erosion of this country's great assets.

My immediate concern is my 'backyard'—the south east forests of NSW, which are rapidly being destroyed to supply woodchips. This is being done under the euphemistic guise of 'integrated logging', which sounds much nicer than 'clear felling'. These days, as a sop to public concern, a few token trees are left standing, poor unprotected reminders of the splendour which once existed, supposedly for seed, and to provide habitat for the thousands of birds and animals whose homes have been destroyed. I just wish that you, and everyone in Australia, could see the awful damage still being done to our forests—the erosion, not just from the logging operations but from the vast network of roads required for logging, the siltation of some of the most beautiful creeks and rivers in the world, and the destruction of so many sensitive, unspoilt areas.

You spoke to a bloke who had travelled around Australia for a year collecting ants for someone to study, and he remarked on how little was known about these creatures. So it is with our forests—very little research has been done, and we are destroying them without even knowing what lives there, and how everything relates.

FROM:
J. SIMMONDS
Wynnum, Qld.

I listen each Sunday morning to the 'Why I Live Where I Live' segment. I would like to say something in defence of surburbia.

I have been fortunate in that I've seen much of Australia. I have been to the far tropics, to Darwin in winter, to Tasmania in autumn, to the west in the spring when the wildflowers stretch to the horizon and over the mountains. But I was always happy to come back to my small suburban home.

I have planted my trees and watched them grow. I take great pleasure in harvesting my citrus fruits and vegetables. My pecan tree turns golden in autumn and reminds me of my Victorian childhood. I have a frangipani at my back door. Its perfume fills the warm summer nights and blossoms litter the lawn. Ring-tailed possums visit the tree. I don't begrudge them what they eat. I have resident blue-tongued and bearded dragon lizards in the yard. The bearded dragons are of all sizes, from tiny young ones to Oscar, the patriarch of the neighbourhood, who has been about for years.

I waken to the sound of many tiny birds twittering in the trees outside my window. Many birds visit my garden during the day. They help maintain a chemical-free garden. I live one hundred yards from the sea. There are no sandy beaches, but there is an abundance of bird life on the tidal flats. It is always a pleasure to stroll along the waterfront.

My home, garden and surroundings please me and I am content. This is why I live where I live, although it is just suburbia.

WHY I LIVE WHERE I LIVE

I live in Broken Hill and have done so for many years now, because that was where my husband came from.

Before we married I lived on the waterfront at Lavender Bay (opposite Luna Park) in Sydney and had the luxury of being able to actually catch fish in the harbour and swim in the wooden-palinged waterfront pools when the tide was high. When it was low we swam outside of them, taking the risk of any sharks being around (of course our parents didn't know—how foolish the young are sometimes).

I also had the luxury of being able to row in a rowboat under the Harbour Bridge and fish from there, as there was nowhere near the amount of craft and ferries that there are today.

I met my husband-to-be while he was holidaying in Sydney and when we married we thought we'd come to Broken Hill (his home town) to save some money for a deposit for a home back in Sydney somewhere, as there was plenty of money to be earned in Broken Hill at that time.

While travelling on the train, the Silver City Comet, which has now unfortunately been put to rest in the train museum, I wondered what I had let myself in for. Mile after mile after mile of sand-hills, desert and salt-bush. I just couldn't imagine how I could possibly live in this town where everyone seemed to be related to so and so's cousin and I was now on my own except for my newly-gained husband, who tried hard to make things better.

I soon got busy, however, having my own family and doing up an older home we purchased, which I considered a palace because it was ours. The only thing wrong? It was right opposite a huge gasometer!

As the years went on, I grew to love the countryside with the red soil and bright orange and red sunsets. We have since built a home with large windows right on top of a hill where we can take full advantage of the splendid sunset every evening.

So, instead of looking out of the window and seeing the harbour waters, Luna Park and the Harbour Bridge, I now look out of the window and see the undulating hills now covered in green, patches of red soil and hundreds of corellas flying in at sundown across the beautiful orange sunset.

I consider myself very lucky to have 'lived where I live' in both cases. PS. It has taken your show to make me appreciate these things. I used to take everything for granted but now when I look I look with different eyes.

These are letters from the children in Year 6/7 at Coorow Primary School. They enjoy listening to your program and hope that you enjoy reading their letters about Coorow.

My name is Holly Croft and I live in a small town called Coorow. Coorow is situated between Carnamah and Moora. I live with my brother, Tristan, Mum, Dad, pet dog Dusty and my pony, Ellie (actually she's lent to me). I really enjoy living in Coorow.

Spring is the best season in Coorow because of all the beautiful wildflowers. There are lots of beautiful places in Coorow to go for picnics.

Coorow is really great because everyone knows everyone else. Our school has eighty-one people in it, each class has about twenty people.

On weekends I ride Elly, make cakes, read, do jobs, eat lollies, play games, and in summer go to the pool and heaps more.

Coorow means 'valley of the mists'. It is an Aboriginal name. My hobbies are horseriding, collecting stamps, stickers and horse pictures.

Overall I love where I live!!!

My name is Joel Loveridge. I am eleven years old and I live with my Mum, who nags a lot, and my sister, who's coming home from Perth this Friday. Which will be a pity because she'll really annoy me about writing to her, which I didn't for two terms. I live where I live because Mum, Jodie and I move around a lot, and Mum works on the land we live on. I go to Coorow School but live in Winchester which is twenty-four km north of Coorow. I travel on the Carnamah High School bus to Coorow so Jodie and I are the only passengers apart from the high school kids. It is fun on the farm because out the back there are some smashed up cars. I also like the farm because the house is old and there's a lot of old bottles around, but I don't like the farm because we've got chickens and every time they kill one I have to bury it.

Hello, my name is Chelsea Croft and I am twelve years old. I live in Coorow, it is situated halfway between Perth and Geraldton. The reason that our family lives in Coorow is because all of our relations lived in Coorow. If you happen to want to know what Coorow stands for it is 'mist in the valley'. Here is some information that would be of some interest to you. When I was young our house burnt down. What happened was this.

My mother went to kindy to pick up Daniel (my brother) from kindy. Our house is sort of near the kindy. She was cooking a roast for tea and the oven caught alight. Where I was sleeping was beside the oven. A lady went past (mother's friend) who was also picking up her child from kindy. She asked my mum if she had her pot belly stove going and mum said, 'No'.

It was the middle of summer and she didn't have the pot belly going so she went home and there was a big crowd standing outside with a lot of smoke pouring from the house . When mum got to the scene she cried out, 'My baby'.

Our neighbour was an Army captain. He kicked down the door and rescued me. It must have been pretty good, it made the front page of the newspaper.

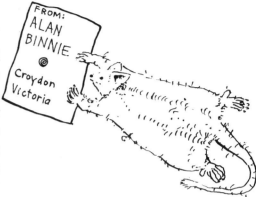

We have recently moved from a cottage in Kilsyth to an archaeological site in Croydon. The site contains a classic 1950s weatherboard house which we are attempting to renovate.

While we are doing this renovation we are scraping away at the outer layers of the house and its walls, and at times we resemble a heads down and bums up group of archaeologists, digging into the past. Let me tell you about some of the things that we have discovered in 'the dig'.

We began by scraping back some wallpaper, the top layer of which was some of that semi-formal stuff from the late 1970s that made little or no social comment at all. Underneath that layer was another batch of wallpaper which was from the late 1960s; flowery and purple with good vibes. Underneath all this wallpaper was the original paint scheme of the 1950s—bold and confident and unsophisticated in its design.

The existing light fittings are a mixed bag. There is the upside-down green wine bottle that hangs in one of the old kids' rooms that has a groovy feel, and in contrast there is the Sunday-best chandelier which hangs in the lounge room for all to see.

There is the extension that was built when the third son was born and the parents soon realised that three boys would not be able to share the existing space and play indoors in mid-winter without causing grievous damage to the house and the other inhabitants.

Out in the yard you can still see the small side gate that the kids would have used to share the neighbours' cubby house and a lemonade in the summer heat. Or you can see where the pampas grass plant was (before I spent hours of sweat and three trips to the tip to remove it). This was the popular idea of garden decoration before we discovered the beauty of the grevillea!

And so we dig and scrape away at our new home and get a chance to see a small bit of Australia's history.

Listening to your program this morning brought back a flood of childhood memories, and for the first time gave me the urge to put pen to paper and write to tell someone about 'where I live'.

No, I was not born in the country, nor do I live there now. I was born in a suburb of Sydney, on the banks of the old Parramatta River. We had a waterfront home and what seemed to me as a small child acres of open spaces. Our playground was the river and its shoreline. On both sides of our home there were vacant blocks of land known to us as 'paddocks'. One of these had the sandstone foundations of a home that was never built, and as the land was sloped there was one section one-storey high. This was our fortress! So many battles were won and lost there, so many acts of bravery performed from the heights of its fortress wall, and so many great picnics!

Our adventures were just through the hole in the paling fence, or at the end of the garden in the muddy shores of the river—trawling for prawns at night, which was done by walking knee high in water, pulling the bassinette net between us; sailing our raft (an old refrigerator door with a dahlia pole for a mast and Mum's yellow dress as a sail) and Buster (the sheep); or building the annual bonfire in one of the 'paddocks' or, in later years, in the river itself because they were so large.(these were done with the help of all the neighbours who saved up their tree loppings, tyres, etc for months beforehand.); having rowing races in our dinghy with the GPS eights, or exploring the timber stacks up river or the derelict barges in the bay; watching the magnificent sunsets across the mangroves on the other side of the bay, or the early morning sun glistening off the water just in front of the house. Only a few of the hundreds of memories I have of 'where I lived'.

A true kids' paradise—entertainment around every corner—and a very understanding Mum in the kitchen.

I enjoy it when you read people's poems about 'Why I like to live where I live'.

Since I have lived in the country for most of my life I appreciate how beautiful our suburban block is. We live on the corner of a school block, so are surrounded by native bush. We have no fences and therefore a limitless garden. We have no neighbours, except across the road.

Perhaps you would like to read my poem. I hope you like it. (I am 21 years old.)

Oasis

Nine or ten ancient tuarts guard our house like giants over a palace.
Immaculate lawns stretch over the two acres, resembling the St Andrews Golf Course.

THE AAO STUDIO IN CERAMICS

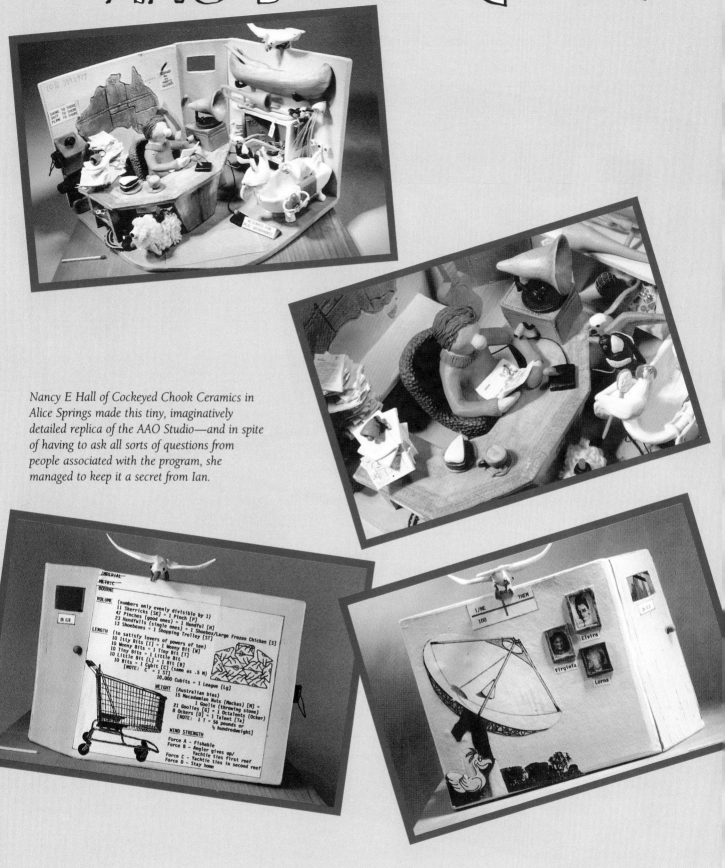

Nancy E Hall of Cockeyed Chook Ceramics in Alice Springs made this tiny, imaginatively detailed replica of the AAO Studio—and in spite of having to ask all sorts of questions from people associated with the program, she managed to keep it a secret from Ian.

THOSE SHOPPING TROLLEYS...
OPEN DAY AT SALE

Shopping trolleys have lives of their own . . .
here's one in the bush near Daly River in the
Northern Territory and another in a junk yard
at Guildford.

During the ABC's Open Day at Sale in Victoria,
Ian signed autographs but was sometimes
obscured from view by a large group of fans.

Australia All Over Goes All Over

Shown here preparing the program on location at the Longyard Hotel in Tamworth (Country Music Festival 1988), Ian gets photos from listeners reflecting all kinds of activities, such as a show exhibit taking the program as its theme, and Nigel Scullin's unusual mackerel bait in the Gulf . . . he uses maracas that he won and that are replicas of Peter Allen's.

BEAUTIFUL WILDERNESS

This photograph by Ralph Lindsay shows Island Head Creek and Port Clinton, part of the beautiful Shoalwater Byfield Wilderness area of central Queensland . . .

. . . and here is Ian in a relaxed moment.

Numerous fruit trees and vines deliver foods fit for a king all summer long.
The Australian native eucalypts, colourful roses and exotic fruit trees hide the old house from the road.

I race, and jump, and play in this endless garden, like a princess, or a fairy;
As only such deserves this oasis in the cement city.

Relaxing in the hammock, under the Japanese pepper tree, it is easy to drift off into dreamworld,

Totally untouched by the forty degree heat that the rest of the city swelters in.

The early morning songs of magpies, honey-eaters and 'twenty-eights'
Effectively drown out the impatient drone of the ever-increasing peak-hour traffic.

Superbly situated within walking distance to several schools and shops.

Who would believe the capital city of Western Australia is only twenty to thirty minutes away by car, bus and bicycle?

Through these eyes, 'my place' is a palace set in an oasis of beautiful gardens contrasting with the surrounding concrete desert.

This is why I like to live where I live.

I thought you might like this poem I wrote after a night spent battling the bugs.

FROM:
KATE BIDDLECOMBE
Broome, Western Australia

Bugs!

There's bugs up in my bedroom
There's bugs out in the hall
There's no place in this whole darned house
That has no bugs at all.

The pest man came to spray them
It didn't take him long
I went out for the whole day
'Cos I couldn't stand the pong!

Two weeks later they were back
Crawling on the sink
Great big bugs, as large as life
And looking 'in the pink'.

My nerves they were in tatters
I tried everything to foil them
Then I thought of the old saying
'If you can't beat 'em, join 'em.'

So I grew an extra set of limbs
My wings are brown and shiny
Antennae grow out of my head
My legs are long and spiny.

The next time that you aim a blow
At any bug you see,
Take a longer, closer look
For that bug might be ME!

The bugs do grow big up here in Broome—you know, the big flying cockroaches. The average size is about two inches long. Sometimes at night the verandah and front path are just a seething mass of bugs. My dog, Ziggy, has a great time crunching them (makes me feel sick)! Perhaps a better name for him would be 'Bug Breath'!

Despite the bugs, I love living in Broome. We've been here six years and I would hate to live anywhere else! The climate suits us well, even the 'troppo' season. Not much rain this 'wet' though, looks like the east copped it all again. Thought we might get a few showers rom your namesake 'cyclone Ian' as it passed by, but no such luck. Two weeks ago, though, we had one of our famous 'isolated thunderstorms', lightning struck the house and blew the colour telly up, and the phone went out as well! Fortunately we have a six-inch black and white telly, so the kids can still watch their favourite programs without too much whingeing.

I am an Anglican priest. I have left the regular parish ministry in order to live in the Bulloo Shire which covers the 73 000 square kms (28 000 square miles) of SW Queensland. I came with one change of clothes, no money, no car and no house—just as the Bible says clergymen should.

I have never been so content, so fulfilled, so rich or so free. Each evening I go bush walking down the banks of the Bulloo River, disturbing the abundant animal life. There must be dozens of places like this around the interior of Australia that have never had a resident minister of any church. And they are just waiting to make other clergy as content as I am.

Hope you enjoy the poem I wrote—careful as you read it, the speed changes suddenly and deliberately!

PS. Would you believe I see every family in this vast area each couple of months. I go with the police and with the mail trucks. And my church notes go out to every family with the school newsletter. This must be the only parish run on zero dollars, just for the love of it!

WHY I LIVE WHERE I LIVE

Keith's Poem

In the morning
In the bushland
In the sunshine oven heat
See the opal cutter searching in the rocks beneath his feet.
Raise the arm and raise the hammer
Pitting strength against the stone
Feels the jarring, feels the stopping
Feels his flesh against the bone

Raised the eyebrows
Raised the forehead
Matted hair against the hat
See the emus walking slowly
Silent, haughty like a cat.
Comes a whirling
Shaking bushland
See the leaves on moving trees
'Send it here, Lord,' whispers cutter
'I can take its cooling breeze.'

In the morning, in the noonday,
Through the evening's angled rays
Works the cutter, tiring shoulders,
Blurring stone before him plays
Slinging eyes with salty moisture
Fuzz the sight he strains to use
Then he glimpses smoky opal
Holds it in his hand to muse

I thought you might like to know 'Why I Live Where I Live'.

As a young man I had the fortune of travelling overseas through many different cultures, landscapes and climate zones. When Marge (friend, companion and wife) and I were looking for land we looked for a climate where we could grow mangoes and pawpaws, live near the rainforest, enjoy peace and quiet.

FROM:
KEITH JAFFRAY
Byfield
Queensland

We ended up in Byfield, forty kilometres north of Yeppoon, just inside the Tropic of Capricorn, in the hinterland of the Capricorn Coast.

Here it was—the end of the road, the least populated area on the east coast of Australia, an extraordinary sub-tropical climate, magnificent forest...a true paradise on earth!

We live 1000 feet above sea level on a plateau in the foothills of the Coast Range, nine miles from the sea. We are on the edge of the Shoalwater/Byfield Wilderness—the largest and most diverse wilderness on the east coast of Australia outside of Cape York. Behind our house is Mt. Bayfield (1950 ft) part of the rugged Coast Range, clad in open eucalypt forest. At about 1300 ft the forest dramatically changes into rainforest, the southernmost pocket of true tropical rainforest in Queensland. This rainforest wilderness literally surrounds our house.

To the east we have an open view over the coastal plain—wallum country interspersed with swamps and swift-flowing creeks, to huge and ancient coastal sand dunes clad in coastal heath, some up to 225 meters high. Beyond the dunes we look out over the deep blue Coral Sea to the Keppel Islands.

The Shoalwater/Byfield Wilderness exists in an area known as a crossover zone. This area is characterised by being the northernmost limit for many temperate species of flora and fauna, the southernmost limit for many tropical species of flora and fauna, the home to many sub-tropical species, as well as being a stopover point for many migratory birds and sea creatures. Over thirty percent of land mammals and thirty-five percent of all Australian bird species are found here.

The variability of land form types, topography, aspect and therefore microclimates gives the Shoalwater/Byfield Wilderness (some 300 000 hectares) its claim to recognition as one of the world's great natural masterpieces.

Marge and I, along with our three kids, have created our own lifestyle here with the wilderness. We run a certified organic farm and supply southern markets. We feel privileged to be able to boast clean air, water and soil, and are proud to be part of a sustainable industry.

FROM:
ERIC KROLL
Tresswell State School
via Springsure
Queensland

I live where I live because that's where I have been put. I teach at Tresswell State School. It is situated 1000 kilometres north-west of the nearest ABC Shop (Brisbane).

After school hours the population is one man and a dog. The dog is mine and is called Bunji. One half of the twain lives in the dogbox and the other half lives in the garage.

My friends told me when I was sent here that in two weeks I'd be talking to myself. I got the dog so that if the Inspector asks me if I have started talking to myself I can say 'No'.

Since I arrived at my dog box on January 9th I have had three visitors:
1 A friend
2 A bloke who was lost, and
3 A drunk. The pace never slackens off.

My dog thinks I'm sick, so no tea for Bunji tonight. Bunji keeps me from going insane despite what my analyst says. He doesn't even believe I can colour in the skin on the inside of my dog's ears with a paintbrush.

And that's why I live where I live.

Yours in stability

PS. I can have the radio up as loud as I like. The dog doesn't object.

It's unlikely that Eric Kroll is sane. Generations of careful genetic engineering can't have gone so badly wrong. This belief that he is sane comes from the reassurances the pixies give him.

Thank you for your letter. I'm infuriated with Macca for demanding everyone write to me and am *suing*. Bunji has had a nervous breakdown (after I forced her to drink a bottle of after-shave which was given to me for my birthday and which I never use and didn't want). She is climbing trees and hanging by her rear claws from the uppermost branches. I believe she thinks she is a flying fox.

Yours in sanity

How are you? I'm fine. I have to write to you because Eric (Mr Kroll) can't answer all his letters. Eric (Mr Kroll) is my teacher. I come to school on a bus. I live in Queensland. My name is Kellie Maree Roberts. I am eight years old. I am in grade three. There are twelve children in the whole school. Eric (Mr Kroll) is a good teacher.

More than twelve years ago I received an Education Department telegram which instructed me to take up a secondary teaching appointment in the Riverina. At the time I was numbed with shock because I'd been certain of a Western Suburbs appointment, and I was very reluctant to give up a busy inner-city lifestyle for the rural unknown.

The first six months were gruelling. In Sydney I'd taught Italian to eager adults, and the contrast of this experience with the horror of adolescents in the classroom was extreme. I discovered that most children have little in common with Rousseau's noble savage—they were out to test me and I soon learned my limitations! I also learned to love the flat, brown landscape and the vast, cloudless sky. The rows of vines and orange trees were a memory of Italy and the dry heat proved to be far less debilitating than the coastal humidity. My parents had begun their lengthy courtship in Narrandera and my father had dug graves and enlisted in the Army in 1939 in Griffith. My return to the Riverina appealed to them immeasurably. I was able to visit locations that were part of family lore and I met distant cousins in the school playground.

During the first four years in Griffith I lived in a flat in the centre of town. Then I purchased a block of land at Yenda and had a prefabricated house erected. Now the house is surrounded by a jungle garden of grevilleas, fruit trees and flowers. The rich soil performs miracles, although I don't have as much time or energy as I'd like to keep the garden under control. Teaching is a profession that demands more effort each year—perhaps middle-age has sapped my vitality!

Yenda mornings are marvellous. The bright dawn quietness is shattered by panicky explosions of galahs overhead and soothed by the light wings of ibises. Country life can be daunting: sometimes I'm the prey of dogs and geese, and there's the summer threat of snakes. But the night sky is clear and boundless, full of mysteries and truths. And although I still need the occasional city fix of films, friends and bookshops, I wouldn't choose to live in any other house in any other town.

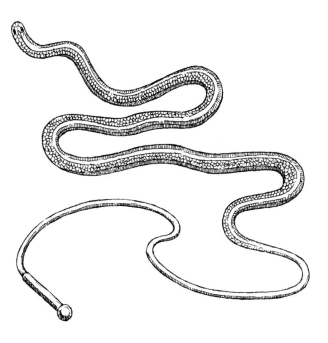

ABORIGINAL NAMES

When you think that Aboriginal Australians have been here for more than 40 000 years and Europeans have been here for about 200, you realise how little we know and how much we have to learn. Aboriginal culture enriches Australia—in fact, it defines Australia more than anything else. The words of John Ashe's song, 'Aboriginal Names', which I included on one of my *Australia All Over* records, say it all:

But then what sets us all apart, gives us our natural possie,
Are the rhythmical, beautiful, wonderful names
Of our Aboriginal Aussie
The original, Aboriginal Australians who gave us
Cootamundra, Illawarra . . .

A lot of people send us books they've written. Sometimes it's poetry, or the story of their town or their own story—things which they feel should be written down. One we particularly liked was from Jean Hamilton, an Aborigine from Coonamble. She called her book *Just Lovely*:

'My big brother thought I was just lovely, so that was my
nickname for many years. Brother George would carry me
about on his shoulders. I was a spoilt little brat, when I
think about it now . . .'

Joan and I had a long chat on the program and I learnt a lot about what it was like for an Aborigine to grow up in a country town: no school (her father didn't believe in them), but hunting, crayfishing, rabbiting and picking up bush lore. Sadly, Brother George was lost in the war, and we talked about the unsung number of Aboriginal servicemen who served their country, especially in World War II.

FROM:
ALEX FREEMAN
Terowie, South Aust.

There was a bit in your program about Coorow town's Aboriginal meaning being 'valley of the mist', or something.

Well, I went to Coorow State School for eight years. My grandmother's name was Granny Latham. She was a half-caste and she told me Coorow's Aboriginal name means 'shallow water'. This could be correct as you could dig down about six or seven feet in the sand plain area and get water at that depth.

I'm one-eighth caste. My grandfather was a pioneer of Coorow, and there's a town named after him on the other line (Latham). He leased over 300 000 acres around the place—that's equal to about 148 square miles, a fair chunk of land!

FROM:
STEVE SYMONDS
Newtown, NSW

When Governor Phillip arrived in Australia he brought with him a list of words collected by his friend, Joseph Banks. Banks had collected this native vocabulary on what is now the Endeavour River during the period the Endeavour was beached there for repairs after it was holed on the Barrier Reef. Phillip tried out this vocabulary on the people in the Sydney area and was surprised that they understood none of it— in fact they thought that 'kangaroo' was an English word meaning 'large edible animal' and called cows and sheep kangaroos.

Phillip gradually learnt some of the language of the local people. During an exploration of the Hawkesbury River he met some of the people who lived on the other side of the river. These people, although they understood the language Phillip used, had another language that they used among themselves. Phillip wrote to Banks telling him of his discovery. The reason Banks's collection was not understood in Sydney was because it was a different language.

Banks had collected words in Guugu Yimidhirr while Phillip had learnt Dharruk from the Sydney area and encountered Awabakal from the Hunter area. There were, in fact, about 250 different languages being spoken in Australia at the time Phillip arrived with possibly four times as many dialects of those languages.

We have lost well over a hundred of these languages today and will lose many more in the next ten to twenty years. Dharruk became extinct a long time ago, although we still use Dharruk words today; dingo (domestic dog), warrigal (wild dog), gin (woman), gunyah (humpty), boomerang and Womerah are all from Dharruk.

Australia All Over is heard right across the country and is listened to in many areas where people still speak their own languages, having English as a second language. If we are too lazy to respect the individuality of these languages we are denigrating not only the language but the speakers as well. Some people will argue that it is too difficult to pronounce some of the names. This is possibly true, but if we can learn to pronounce Sioux, Apache, Tlingit and Arapaho from North America, surely we can learn to pronounce Arrernte, Warlpiri, Dharawal and Gamilaraay from our own country?

It was great to hear about the Murray cod on *Australia All Over*. The fish is part of a natural heritage and it's a shame to see them becoming scarce. Environmental pressures—especially the chemicals used in cotton growing—together with overfishing, have taken their toll.

You might be interested to know that although the name Murray cod is firmly entrenched in Australian folklore there are growing references to the fish as goodoo—an Aboriginal name pronounced goo-du. There are shades of barramundi here. Twenty years ago text books still referred to the barra as 'the giant perch' or the 'Palmer perch'—so named after the North Queensland river so graphically dealt with in Hector Holthouse's book *River of Gold*. Since those times barramundi—another Aboriginal name meaning fish with big scales—has universally prevailed.

FROM:
ROD HARRISON
Bribie Island
Queensland

From: JANET E.A. ELDER Casuarina, NT

For a long time I've been wanting to write to tell you how much I enjoy the program but I've never got round to it. However, today's program did it! You talked about Geelong, and the Wool Museum there.

I love the wool industry. I was brought up in the country and one of my greatest pleasures as a child was to watch the shearing. If Dad let me sweep the floor after each shearer had completed a sheep I thought life was wonderful! The smell of the wool, the bleating of sheep, the constant buzz of the shearing machines, and the sight of the beautiful soft white fleeces always thrilled me. My mother had a spinning wheel and taught me how to spin.

When I was a teenager we moved to Geelong. I loved Geelong. It was a rural city in spite of being big and industrial as well. On wool sale days all the brokers' buildings had flags flying to indicate the wool sales were on.

Eventually I moved to work in the Northern Territory, where I've been ever since. Although it is too hot in Darwin to wear wool I still do my hand spinning. When I was teaching Aboriginal women English they taught me many things, one being how they extracted the dye from certain native plants to dye the bark string for their dilly bags and baskets. This led me to experiment by dyeing hand-spun wool with those native dyes and I had excellent results. So the Aboriginal women started me on an exciting new hobby and enabled me to keep in touch with the wonderful wool industry, even though I live in the tropics.

Thanks, Ian, for taking me back to the good old days in Geelong.

RABBITS

Some time ago I had a call from Pam Cooke from South Australia. 'I hear you talking on the program every week about rabbits,' she said, 'so I thought I'd tell you about my husband, Brian, who's in Spain chasing fleas at the moment, and how some time down the track this might help solve our rabbit problem.'

Spanish fleas might help our rabbit problem?

Pam went on to tell me that in the 1960s the CSIRO introduced a rabbit flea from England to help spread myxomatosis, but our hot pastoral country was too much for the little English flea and it just curled up its toes and died. But it seems that there are several fleas in Spain that live on rabbits and spread myxomatosis and Brian was trying to find out if it would be safe to introduce them to Australia. We want fleas that breed on rabbits only and won't spread to any of our other native animals.

Well, after six months Brian came back and we had a chat about his Spanish fleas. I asked if he was hopeful that they'd solve our rabbit problem. 'I think that most of these biological controls, even when they work, are only temporary,' he said, 'because eventually the rabbits develop resistance to whatever you throw at them. But it'll give us a breathing space until we develop the next idea. I've just been up the north-east and rabbit numbers are just colossal there—they're eating vast holes in the country and devastating it. I haven't seen numbers like these since the '60s.'

I asked him if he thought the governments realise how serious the problem is.

'I don't really think the commitment's there that should be, because there's no two ways about it, the rabbits are tearing the guts out of Central Australia and it will take a long, long time to repair the damage. Rabbits have only been there for a little over a hundred years and they've changed the whole landscape.'

*Shooters in the Western District still get a living
from rabbits though their style is a bit different from
the trappers of the past.*

Regarding the rabbit plague in the Simpson Desert: I live adjacent to a large War Service Land Settlement area which was developed in the mid 1950s. Part of this area was infested with rabbits, and I remember driving through it and literally seeing more rabbit ears than blades of grass! They had to be got rid of, and the Gnowangerup Shire was one of the first to introduce the myxomatosis virus into Australia. This resulted in the sudden death of thousands and thousands of rabbits and even today we occasionally see a rabbit suffering from the virus, although it appears they have mostly become immune to it.

For many of us it was the end of the delicious meal of braised rabbit.

Last year I read that Akubra hat manufacturers were having difficulty obtaining enough rabbit furs for their industry. If, as stated by your caller, myxomatosis is not in the area mentioned, why haven't the rabbit trappers again got the industry going? Surely there is a great opening for this market of non-fat meat. It was not uncommon forty to fifty years ago to see truck loads of rabbits being transported to the processors. With today's modern transports this should not be a problem, and it would help to control the rabbit as well as assist in feeding some of the hungry people of the world.

I love your program, as well as rabbit stew!!

I listened with interest to the South Australian proposal to fund a rabbit eradication scheme.

As a former Victorian dairy farmer, and having first hand knowledge of the devastation that rabbits are capable of, the thought occurred to me of a means to finance such a scheme.

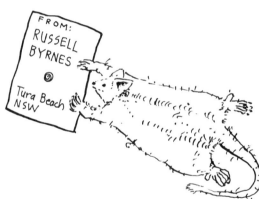

For years farmers and graziers have paid into a cattle and swine compensation fund which has grown into millions of dollars in each state. (For each animal sold a compulsory fee is charged and automatically deducted from sales.)

I believe the NSW Government is proposing $9 million of this fund be taken into consolidated revenue. Surely this money (farmers' money) could be siphoned back for eradication of rabbits to the benefit of all landowners and National Parks.

The wild rabbit in Australia is evolving to become better adapted to our environment. These changes are quite clear even though rabbits have been here for little more than one hundred years.

In some dry, sandhill country in north-east South Australia up to thirty per cent of rabbits are 'sandy' or 'yellow'. If you look at rabbit hair closely you will see that the 'normal' colour is made up by bands of black,

brown and yellow along the shaft of each hair. Yellow rabbits simply lack the enzyme which forms the black and brown pigments and as a consequence have only the yellow band. These yellow rabbits seem to blend in with the sandy soils in many areas. Also, their coats may reflect heat well and this would give them a further advantage.

Rabbits in inland areas generally appear to be lighter in colour than their wet-country cousins. CSIRO scientists showed that this was because the yellow band on the fur is wide and the dark bands are narrow in 'inland' rabbits. In some wet parts of Tasmania up to forty per cent of rabbits are black, so 'evolution' is going in the opposite direction there! No doubt the Tasmanian rabbits are responding to different climatic stresses to those found in inland Australia.

Wild rabbits are occasionally seen with other coat colours or patterns. 'Dutch' or 'dutch collar' is often seen. These rabbits have a white collar or sometimes a white shoulder or white on the face with blue eyes! Albinos are rare. I have only seen two or three in twenty-five years of rabbit shooting.

FROM:
NYE EVANS
Launceston

Tasmania

My solution to the rabbit problem is for Australians to take to eating the little blighters and to using their fur more frequently.

Quite frankly, the sheep is letting us down and in any case its meat is too fatty and full of cholesterol.

It is difficult to convince Australians that there is anything wrong with the land when there is a huge over production of sheep and millions will have to be destroyed this year.

If each Australian family ate at least one rabbit each week that would get rid of about forty million a year and we would all be healthier for it.

The rabbit has proved itself to be the best survivor in our world and we should respect it and start using it because it won't let us down. All these starving people in other parts of the world could be fed Australian rabbit. We could can the bunny and set up quite a lucrative export trade—better than sheep. The texture of rabbit fur is much more pleasant than wool, anyway.

My grandfather, Tom Evans, lived in Sherbourne, Dorset, England, and was a cunning bunny napper. He was always poaching rabbits from the local estates. One morning the local constable apprehended him with ninety-two rabbits strapped to his push bike. Perhaps this should go into the Guinness book of records!

P.S. What about a prize for the first to bring in 100 rabbits strapped to his push bike?

RABBITS

FROM:
BERT GRIFFITHS
Coonabarabran
NSW

From time to time on the program, and elsewhere for that matter, our little furry character Brer Rabbit comes under very heavy fire and, without attempting to defend the indefensible, there must be many, many thousands of other Australians who share a sneaking appreciation for this little fellow— in particular for the way he contributed to the family larder during difficult years, since without him many people would have shared the fate of Mother Hubbard's dog.

I was raised at Ramsgate (a suburb of Sydney) during the depression and it now seems incredible that in those days there existed fairly large areas of scrub, swamp and wild beach front fairly well populated by Brer himself.

With rabbits as my quarry and armed with my gear (an aged ginger ferret with pink eyes and the foulest of tempers, plus a dozen or so home-made nets) I would set out with as much planning as D-Day in Europe.

A full-sized plump rabbit earned me sixpence, and a sale took me to the flicks on Saturday arvo and enabled me to have a professional haircut instead of the candle and bowl that were part of the basin crop my father dished out.

Eventually my efforts paid off. I saved enough to buy an old bike for ten shillings, enabling me to extend my hunting ground to what is now Beverley Hills, Kingsgrove, Roselands and many other suburbs which in those days were just scrub.

Many modern residents sitting by the pool in the manicured gardens of their mansions could not even imagine a young lad with a cranky ferret and a bomb of a bike wandering freely through their area before progress took over.

Meanwhile we ate rabbit!

Poor old Mum served them boiled, baked, fried, stewed, curried, hot, cold, sliced, minced and turned into patties, to say nothing of pies and soups. Needless to say we took them with us for lunch, sliced on bread and sometimes even a whole leg.

So the rabbit has my appreciation for its help in times of hardship. Sometimes one should salute a valiant enemy!

Perhaps Head Office was toughening us up for even more trying times to follow a few years later.

Every year Ramsgate and many other suburbs disappeared under a huge canopy of vines which took over fences, chook runs, lattice-work, backyards and any other available space on vacant land.

They were, of course, choko vines, on which grew millions of big green chokos covered with spikes like pins and a taste like wet paper. Yes, you are right—they were the perfect companion for rabbit. So we ate them.

We had rabbit and choko or choko and rabbit, again boiled, baked, fried, whole, halved, sliced and in a thousand ways.

Breakfast might be fried choko on toast or mashed choko bubble and squeak, and lunch could produce some snifter surprises such as choko and beetroot sandwiches.

Evening meals always included our humble mates, even to the dessert. Choko cooked with beetroot takes on a pinkish colour and when halved and sweetened was served up as stewed pears. Diced, they made the basis for fruit salad.

If you can bear it, let's move to the condiment department. This included choko pickles and chutney both sweet and sour in a host of combinations. They also kept well and assured a supply of choko flavour during the winter until spring brought fresh supplies. Once my father did his melon and threw the pickles to the chooks who, having picked at them, never laid again.

Our jam assortment, to mention a few, included, choko and rhubarb, choko and passionfruit, choko and loquat and choko with any kind of fruit. I could always swap a rabbit for a bucket of fruit. But to my mind the jam par excellence—wait for it—was choko and prickly pear fruit! Rugged stuff mate—rugged! We had a technique for removing the prickles from the pears by dropping them into a sugar bag and rubbing them clean from the outside.

And that raises another question—how do we manage without that prince of carry-alls, the sugar bag? Supreme for fishing, camping, mushrooming, shopping and for making peg-bags, aprons, cowboy suits and a thousand uses—even as wet weather gear.

Finally, I did not intend to waffle on like this when I started—sorry about that—I just wanted to tell you how much we enjoy listening to your philosophy on life and the importance of simple, natural things.

FROM:
VERCO COOK
Esperance
Western Australia

I'm a sixty-one year old bush cocky who has spent a lifetime loving our beautiful country. The discussion on feral cats has spurred me to write.

I believe that if we add cats to the endless list of enemies of the environment along with dingoes, rabbits, the Bathurst burr, skeleton weed and a thousand others, we are in danger of over-simplifying. This is a mistake we often make in our approach to the environment. We need to visualise the whole country as a national park. The term 'balance of nature' has been around for a long time and can't be avoided. The Aboriginals saw this, and so must we.

The feral cat problem has arisen mainly as a result of the explosion

in numbers of other creatures. Action is certainly needed, but what?

Cats eat rabbits, those destroyers of the Australian environment. Cats do not destroy the very habitat of the environment, the scrub, forest and heath. But rabbits do. I recently spent five months on the Nullarbor and jogged every morning through the dying remains of that vast and beautiful area. Rabbit warrens, all occupied and of great age, occur on an average of one hundred metres apart in every direction for thousands of kilometres. I searched in vain for a single surviving new generation mallee tree; the dead and dying remains of the old mallees stretched away to the far horizon. All regeneration of mallees, casuarina, and all palatable-to-rabbits species has ceased. Of course, sheep and kangaroos also graze on those stations but their numbers are controlled by man. Not so with Brer Rabbit. Pussy is doing a grand job for Australia in the absence of the rabbit's natural predators, the badger and others.

Left to herself, Nature will come up with the optimum total of living substances on a given area and keep it in a measure of equilibrium. Only man, of all the creatures, is capable of threatening this process by removing predators, by introducing prey without its predator. In Australia we have done this on a massive scale. Much of what we are doing treats only one part of the problem and ends up creating others.

In 1949 I was a girl in London at my first job—a pupil cook at the Southwestern Hospital for Incurable Diseases. The hospital had 250 beds and the kitchen was overseen by a supervisor we called 'Mother'. Most of the girls were under eighteen.

In post-war England food was still rationed and meat was very short, but four days a week we had Australian rabbit on the menu. The frozen rabbits arrived twice a week in big slatted wooden crates with heads and feet hanging out each end. I did the skinning and jointing and still have the white powder-puff tail of the first rabbit I skinned forty-three years ago! Your program reminded me of that period in my life and I took out my soft white rabbit's tail. Australia played its part at that frugal time in England, the humble rabbit adding a tasty repast to the jaded English table.

I have lived in Australia for forty years and last month I became an Australian citizen. Why become an Australian after all these years? Well, it is a personal affirmation that I am indeed proud to live where I live.

FROM: KITTY JONES
Frankston, Victoria

INTERVIEW

with Bert from Purlewaugh, NSW

'Oh, Macca, it's Bert, from Purlewaugh.'

Where's Purlewaugh?

'Between Coonabarabran and Tambar Springs, about twenty miles out. Listen, mate, somewhere in your gear there you've got a cowbell that you ring.'

Oh, yeah, a little condamine bell.

'I want to have a bit of a grizzle about that bell. We're pretty close to the road here and we've got two Great Danes—affable blokes—they deter a lot of people. To give 'em a bit of a hand I tie a cowbell on the front gate and when people ring it those dogs go down there to say g'day and go beserk. Now the other morning you rang that bell without warning and the transistor disappeared from beside the bed, went round the yard and got torn to shreds. Thank you—that's one you owe me! And a couple of weeks later, without any warning, you rang it again. I chased the dog around the yard in my pyjamas and I got that one back. It's mutilated, but it works. You owe me one and a half transistors and a promise that in future, mate, you won't ring the damn thing, or you'll give a little warning so I can turn the volume down. I can't stand the expense!'

Look, I'm sorry about that, Bert. How long have you been in Purlewaugh?

'About fourteen years.'

And do you know how it got the name Purlewaugh?

'It means "a place of many birds".'

A place of many birds . . . and a place of torn-up transistors.

'Yeah, and cranky old fellas. I know you travel a fair bit. If you come past here I suggest you accelerate as you go past.'

And don't ring any bells.

'And don't ring any bells! Keep up the good work, mate.'

All right, Bert; thanks for calling, and I owe you one and a half.

SIGNS OF RAIN

Everyone has a particular sign of rain, whether it's an aching bunion or a freshly washed car. In 1990, Phil, from Nevertire in central western New South Wales, phoned in to tell us that he reckons carpet snakes can be an infallible sign of a big rainfall:

'Last year we had twelve inches,' Phil said, 'the biggest fall since the '50s, and the day before I was goin' down the highway here and I saw this big carpet snake. I'm tryin' to get him off the road 'cause I knew he was goin' to get run over, and I'm there pokin' him off when these fellas come down the road at about a hundred miles an hour and ran over the end of him, but I got him off and he seemed to be OK. Then it was the followin' night we got the twelve inches of rain. Anyway, blimey, last week I was going up the paddock to do a bit of work on the tractor and here's this other big carpet snake, and I got a stick and tried to poke him off the road but all he wanted to do was look at me and talk. Ended up I got a bigger stick and moved him but all he did was lie there, so I went away and did my work. Started rainin' that night and since then we've had ten-and-a-half inches, so you can't tell me they don't know what's goin' on!'

Carpet snakes, eh? Well, there you go! I told Phil about the night I did a concert at Glen Innes in New South Wales and we were talking about signs of rain and a lady up on the balcony said, 'Yoo-hoo, Ian! My name's Lorna and I know it's going to rain when my cat sleeps on its head'.

Phil and I agreed we'd rather rely on the snakes.

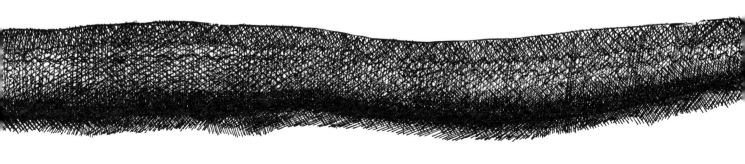

FROM:
CHARLES TYSON
Springsure, Queensland

A few weeks ago I heard you talking about wildlife pointers to the weather. A couple of these that I have been brought up with are: kookaburras laughing between noon and 2 pm means rain within three days; the cat washing behind both ears should mean an inch of rain.

However, this year I have seen something that seems to me to be an even more important sign. We keep our gumboots on the back verandah near the kitchen door. Early this year I heard croaking coming from there and found that a large green frog had taken up residence. I reckon that if the frogs have taken to wearing gumboots it should mean floods are coming! Sure enough, in the first first two months of this year we have had as much rain as in the last eighteen months!

SIGNS OF RAIN

'Go to the ant, thou sluggard, consider their ways and be wise.' This is very true: we can learn a lot by watching the animals and birds.

We lived for a time in flood area in South Grafton. We had an old shed in the yard and it was a habit to go and see just how far the ants would travel up the wall. The higher they got was an indication of how high the water would be in flood time. Also there was a dry creek bed across the road and when floods were predicted we would nearly be driven crazy with the croaking of hundreds of frogs trying to outdo one another.

Whilst working on our property here on the head of the Barrington River, the weather is usually referred to many times a day—a habit of most country people. We generally notice all the old signs such as black cockatoos flying up-river, a dog lying on his back with his legs in the air, the apple trees flowering, or a horse lying flat out in the sun, but these generally fail to bring rain to our property.

The ants—well they're different! My brother swears by them as rain indicators; however, I'm not convinced that they tell whether it is going to rain tomorrow, next week or next month. But they are at least as accurate as the professional weather forecasters. Our father's observation is the most foolproof. He believes the best sign of rain is in the form of sap frothing at the base of a gum tree—you've had three or four inches of rain by then!

We've just survived a local flooding situation up here in comparative comfort—we are lucky. We live on the northern slopes of the Liverpool Range so water drains away fairly fast and we don't have the Nyngan Plains-type problem, but I knew that floods were coming, so I stocked up on chook food, dog food and human food.

And how did I know? ANTS!

I'd read that the forecasters expected El Nino to break around early April and wouldn't have had February in mind . . . except for our ants.

We live in an old weatherboard homestead, built close to the ground on log bearers, impossible for any pest extermination expert to de-pestify. So the ants move around continually between flooring and ceiling and send out their foraging parties the minute we relax our defences. Their trails appear in the most unlikely places, but we'd never seen any nests inside until the middle of January. I came back from a couple of days away, went into the 'office' to check out neglected paperwork. In that short time the ants had moved in. AND HOW! They had carried their

FROM: JENNY HUDSON
Quirindi NSW

FROM: JAMES LAURIE
Gloucester NSW

FROM: H. WILDMAN
Grafton NSW

eggs onto table and desk and were busy creating new homes between the pages of letters, bills, Christmas cards, within manilla folders, on the table, under the computer, under the base of the screen and printer, and, most disturbingly, within the keyboards. It took hours to de-antify the office.

We had to go to Sydney the next day for ten days. When we returned the house smelt of ants. This time they'd gone into a bedroom. They were carting their eggs above a door lintel; they were under a lamp base at table height; they were nesting in the frame of a mirror at about five feet six inches above.ground— thousands of them. We had to dismantle the mirror and blow them and the eggs out with compressed air.

That's when I was really convinced that we'd not only have rain, we'd have floods! And well before April. So I went to the nearest town and stocked up for a siege. Told the neighbours about it. Some laughed, some got ready. My husband had to return south and he couldn't get back. But we've actually had a comfortable flood up here, with lashings of tucker and a few good books, doing some of the indoor jobs you don't usually do when the outdoors beckons.

Are you aware of the cloud formation known as a 'mackerel sky'? It was originally explained to me by my father fifty years ago. He claimed the cloud formation resembled the scales on the side of the mackerel fish, hence the saying mackerel sky. It quite often heralds the approach of an intense area of low pressure which may or may not produce rain within forty-eight hours. A mackerel sky is a fairly common cloud formation here in north-eastern Victoria, being seen at least three or four times each year.

FROM:
RAY McPHERSON
Benalla Victoria

FROM:
ALLAN KINGHORNE
Cowra, NSW

Years ago I was told by several old timers of a storm bird, or rain bird. The story goes that when this special bird appears it will rain. Over the years I have observed different birds and their behaviour when rain is about. For example, swallows swoop over dry land instead of water, galahs dive and screech ahead of a storm, currawongs disappear when rain or storms are about, and when the weather clears they reappear. But the storm bird or rain bird seems very different as it only appears when rain is about.

Sometimes people write rude letters but I don't like rude people, so I usually write them a rude letter back! Doing *Australia All Over* gives me great job satisfaction and, as you'll see from these letters, there's great listener satisfaction out there, too—and that's what makes me happy in the job.

A Lengthy Sermon

This *true* story came to light at our recent Lions Club dinner and involves a good Lion member, Reverend Kevin Dobson, who, I am sure, would not mind if it were told again.

He was delivering a somewhat lengthy sermon to his congregation when he noticed an elderly lady sitting near the back of the church take a small item from her handbag and place it in her ear.

Always concerned about his flock's response to his sermons, and thinking the ageing parishioner had resorted to using a hearing aid, Reverend Kevin decided to deliver the last two pages of his prepared sermon, which were optional, depending on the reaction of his congregation. He felt heartened when he observed that the dear lady had a gentle and happy smile on her face.

At the end of the service, while greeting his congregation as they left the church, Reverend Kevin told the lady he was delighted that her hearing aid had helped her to hear his message.

'Hearing aid?' she said, 'oh, no, that was my little radio's earpiece. You were so boring today that I tuned into *Australia All Over*!!

FROM: ROBERT EDGAR, Speed, Victoria

From: HELEN EDDIE
Mildura
Victoria

I've been going to write for twelve months or more, but here it is at last!

How satisfying it must be for you to receive many hundreds of letters expressing appreciation for your program. We thank you for the long hours spent in preparation, reading, sorting out letters, music, talking to people—your whole life must revolve around this wonderful program!

Last year my sister, Mrs Bev Tischer from Beerwah, Queensland, was cleaning out her fridge while listening to you. She felt moved to write and express her appreciation as well. Let me tell you she HATES writing letters—I'm lucky to get one per year—so she thinks you're a very special person! When Bev meets a nice person anywhere, eg. a pleasant shop assistant, she says 'I'll bet they listen to Macca!'

And so this is just a note on behalf of thousands of listeners who haven't yet put pen to paper. We thank you for the joy you bring each week; we thank you for your kind and loving thoughts, expressed with humour and humility.

From: TESS WOOLLEY
North Fitzroy
Victoria

I have never before felt like writing to any media personality, but I think it's time to stop being apathetic and put pen to paper.

What I want to say is really quite simple. AUSTRALIA ALL OVER IS THE BEST PIECE OF RADIO ENTERTAINMENT AROUND TODAY! Well, now I've managed to get that piece of important information down on paper I can relax and tell you why: the music is great, it's Australian, it's superb quality, it's interesting and it's fun.

I particularly enjoy listening to the people who ring in or write to you and share with the rest of Australia their experiences about life in their part of this amazing land in which we are lucky enough to live. I have travelled quite extensively throughout Australia and I find myself overwhelmed with my memories whenever a person calls from somewhere I've visited. Last week a man called from north of Albany and I was immediately transported back some ten years and could vividly remember the astounding profusion of spring flowers that grew on the roadsides when I was there. And whenever places such as the Alice, Birdsville or Oodnadatta are mentioned I can recall the heat of the sun, the call of the birds, the rustle of the leaves in the trees and the majestic colours of the earth. We live in a truly colourful and lively and spectacular country, don't we?

But in all honesty, the thing I enjoy most about *Australia All Over* is the presenter. Yes, you! I remember all those years ago when you left the presenter's seat to pursue other avenues, and I remember how wonderful it was when you returned to grace our homes with your inimitable style on Sunday mornings.

AAO Stereo

FROM:
CHARLES DEVINE
Campbells Creek
Victoria

I wakes up Sunday mornin' an' turns on the radio
T'listen t'yer, Macca, puttin' on yer Sunday show
Then I wanders in the kitchen an' switch on the trannie there
T'hear the latest gossip comin' in from everywhere.

The kitchen faces north an' the bedroom's in the south
An' the loo is situated in the middle of the house
In the kitchen an' the bedroom I hears mono radio
But sittin' in the loo it comes through like stereo.

They're must'rin' on the High Plains, there's whales at Warrnambool
With all the rain we've 'ad this year Lake Eyre is nearly full
A call from Fitzroy Crossin' an' news from Kakadu
I hears it all in stereo, sittin' in the loo.

I likes yer taste in music an' I likes the songs y'play
I likes the things y'talks about, I like the things y'say
I listens to yer every Sunday mornin' all year through
An' I hears y'mate, in stereo, sittin' in the loo.

Y'ain't afraid t'speak yer mind, I likes that in a bloke,
Y'talks of our environment an' that's no flamin' joke
Y'talks of trees, of birds an' bees an' conservation too
I hears yer words like pearls of wisdom droppin' in the loo.

Australia All Over

It isn't for the greedy, your status isn't in it,
And no amount of petty cash will buy a single minute
Of *Australia All Over* . . . the true Australian voice
That's loved by all the listeners to McNamara's choice.

FROM:
DOROTHY B WATT
Briagolong, Victoria

He's not impressed by opulence, position, class or rank,
It doesn't matter if you sweep the street or run a bank,
If you can spread a little fun, some knowledge or some news
Or live beyond the last black stump or in a city mews;

He loves to hear from off-beat types, old-timers, even kids,
Artistic, crafty, country-wise and battlers short of quids;
Well-travelled folk and nature buffs and truckies—sailors too,
His interests are widely spread and reach to me and you.

And that is why we listen in and cannot get enough
Of Macca's choice of what's worthwhile . . . the truly
Aussie stuff.

Did you realise that *Australia All Over* is a source of great inspiration? It helped me use some psychology when confronted by the daunting task of establishing a garden from scratch.

Not being the most enthusiastic gardener and handyman I developed the ploy of ranking the work second and regarded listening to *Australia All Over* as my primary source of enjoyment. The tales of early pioneers and their hard lives spurred me on to lay the lawn, paint the palings, manhandle the moss rocks and set up the shed. The variety and interest your program contains has made the most boring jobs bearable.

Being a new Australian, I think the Immigration Department should make it a condition of entry that *Australia All Over* is regarded as compulsive listening for all new Australians. 'Here's your entry permit, mate, and your complimentary *Australia All Over* tape!'

I thought I would tell you a little about my father, David Green. He was born in Leadville, NSW, in 1927, one of seven brothers. At twelve he left home after an argument with his father. He spent the next twelve years working as a stockman or carpenter and entertaining himself by entering cycling races, playing rugby league, boxing professionally or, to impress the girls, diving off the top span of the Goondiwindi bridge.

At twenty-four an accident with an axe brought him to Brisbane for thirteen operations on his leg to remove gangrene. It was here he met my mother, married and started a family. It is interesting to note that he obtained the deposit on their farm by being prepaid for two years' worth of weekend work. He later settled down, working for the local council and running a small hobby farm.

My father and his brothers all suffer from a rare genetic disease which causes gradual blindness from the mid to late twenties (all brothers are now fully blind). He retired about fourteen years ago and is kept occupied by showing poultry and by handling and giving advice on horses to the people who agist horses at the farm.

My reason for writing to you is that he never misses your program. As animals must be fed, on a Sunday morning my father can often be found roaming around the farm with walkman headphones in his ears, listening to your program. At this time, not only is he blind but deaf to the outside world as well, contentedly laughing, singing and listening.

TESTIMONIALS

Australia All Over

I've met some funny folk in my time
No doubt you have too
But nothing like this latest lot
That I've been listening to.
This latest breed of Aussies blue
Without a word of warning
Will wake at six to listen to
Macca on Sunday morning.
What kind of man will climb a mount
Just to hear the show?
What kind of man will spray a chook
And let everybody know?
Who is this guy called Macca
Who sings along for fun?
What is this show they listen to
At the rising of the sun?
They talk of trolleys on the march
Of snakes with tin hats on
Of farms with worms, and quandongs too
And where the whales have gone.
You want to know what's going on
From the outback to the sea
And hear an Aussie song or two
Then listen to Macca, like me.

FROM:
PAULINE HARRIS
Greensborough
Victoria

Portrait of 'Macca'

You've had some requests lately,
For photos, cards or posters.
The reason why we want them is,
We think you are the 'mostest'.

I met you down at Fingal (Tas),
Coal shovelling and all that 'yakka'
I even heard you play and sing,
You really were great, 'Macca'.

I took a photograph of you,
It gave me quite a thrill.
But when I got a look at it,
I really felt quite ill.

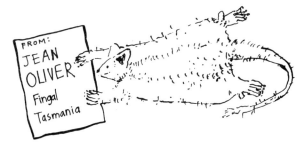

FROM:
JEAN OLIVER
Fingal
Tasmania

The jacket's good, the t-shirt great,
I love your cute chin.
But at the top of the photograph
There's more that should have been.

I don't know how it happened,
The thing I've always dreaded.
Was it me, or the camera shop?
There were you, beheaded.

I went and bought the *Listener*,
It cost two precious dollars.
And when I saw what they had done,
You should have heard my hollers.

Not even the decent photograph,
That I'd been waiting for.
Their photographer is worse than me,
All he can do is draw.

Don't want to be a nuisance,
Don't want to make a fuss.
But all I want is someone,
To take a photograph for us.

Can Jason take a photo,
Or perhaps Virginia will.
And if they won't do that for me,
I'll write to David Hill.

I've helped to push the ratings up,
And now I'm asking PLEASE.
Just get 'Macca' lined up,
And have him saying 'cheese'.

Please get us a photograph,
And end this little matter.
Or do you have a problem too!!
DOES THE CAMERA 'CRACKA' MACCA?

TESTIMONIALS

FROM:
RON STRAHAN
Sofala
NSW

Forgetfulness

My feet hit the floor and I start to get dressed,
The sky's looking cloudy, we could get some rain.
I stand at the window, expanding the chest,
And call out, 'Me Tarzan' and Phyl says, 'Me Jane'.

I turn 'round and smile at her, still snug in bed,
With two big brown eyes peeping over at me.
The only part of her I see is her head,
She's not getting up yet, that's quite plain to see.

I think over all of the jobs for the day,
Like mowing the lawn and then washing the car,
Repairing the fence where it's broken away,
Replacing a string on the Gibson guitar.

I open the door and I go up the back,
Then take a short walk down the road to the bridge,
And when I return, I prepare us a snack,
With rashers of bacon and eggs from the fridge.

I set up a tray, for the one still in bed,
With toast and some marmalade there in a pot,
I pour out some tea for my dear sleepy head,
Put bacon and egg on a plate, piping hot.

I walk to the bedroom with her breakfast tray,
She looks up at me and says, 'Good morning, Ron.
I think you've forgotten what day is today.
It's Sunday, Australia All Over is on.'

I race to the radio, hitting the switch,
My mental processes have never been slacker,
I'm getting so I don't know which day is which,
My mem'ry is failing; forgive me please, Macca.

I felt I should write and say you have achieved something which I don't think has ever been done before on radio in Australia. You have made a place available for so many people to exchange warm greetings and to celebrate their fellow-feeling in the great community of common thought and emotion about our country. As my brother Alan said in a letter to me recently, your program is joyful because it is one where the people of our country share their thoughts with each other; the listeners, to a large extent, *are* the program. If they do happen to disagree

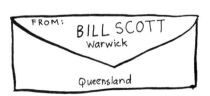

FROM: BILL SCOTT
Warwick

Queensland

at any time we have the satisfaction of knowing that it is an argument within the family, not with an interloper from outside!

This morning, for example, we have listened to two men speak from what must be as far apart as one can get and remain in the country—from the remote south of Tasmania to the island off the north-west coast. Each man was incontestably Australian; they had that common bond which would have let each immediately recognise the other as a brother no matter where in the world they encountered each other!

Speaking as someone who has for most of his life been urging the celebration of our own unmistakable national qualities, let me say how much this delights me.

FROM:
PAMELA GALLAGHER
Toowong, Queensland

Do you realise that Ian McNamara and the program *Australia All Over* are a real health hazard? Once upon a time—seems so long ago—I used to be able to sleep in on Sunday mornings. Now I set my clock-radio to wake me at 5.30 am so I don't miss anything.

How is it that Ian is permitted to air songs that no-one else dares to play? Is it because the ABC is allowed access to real Australians who sing about the lives and loves of dinky-di Australia?

Then there's the effort of having geography lessons when there are messages from places I've never heard of, so I have to *think* as well. And the learning process goes on and on—about our native birds, trees or feral cats. And science! And the proliferation of the ubiquitous shopping trolleys. Do you think that this sort of humour is good for a body every week?

And what about that poetry he reads? Consider all those poets who wouldn't be encouraged to put pen to paper—then *our* culture could wither or be ignored altogether.

On top of that there's the social aspect—instant contact from a woman on a yacht in rough seas, or a group of whale watchers, or steam train enthusiasts who just love the 3801.

Don't you think that explaining some of those typically Australian sporting events is likely to spur our young people on to actually try to achieve something other than being Olympic champions or earning millions of dollars on football fields?

Another thing—are you secretly trying to boost the profits of Telecom as well? Sometimes, often in fact, I am driven to telephoning my brother, who lives in Adelaide and might be doing something sensible like sleeping and dreaming. I feel I have the responsibility of making sure that he doesn't miss instructions about washing chooks, letters from lonely school teachers or auctions of replicas of Peter Allen's maracas.

I first heard *Australia All Over* while visiting a cattle property on the Birdsville Track. I now listen from Logan City. To say that I listen is not quite correct. Normally when a radio is on, I hear it; when the news comes on, I listen; when *Australia All Over* comes on, I am part of it.

No doubt everyone has his or her own reasons for turning in to your (our) show but I think the following ditty sums up mine.

Australia all over; on Sundays we band
With Macca all over our vast family land
From the streets of our cities to dry desert sand
Australia our family, our continent spanned.

What brings us together like families of old?
Perhaps it's the sharing of yarns that are told
Perhaps it's the caring when bad times unfold
We're part of a family, we're part of its mould.

I sometimes wonder how other people listen to your program. Most of us listen in bed or at breakfast, etc., but I expect there must be some folk listening in very strange places or circumstances.

That Radio Show

We listen in the bedroom and we listen in the loo;
We take you to the milking shed and sing along on cue.
The goats appear quite mesmerised but listen without fear
As someone gets a hundred runs and all the neighbours cheer.
The chooks stand round the open door with bright and beady eyes
While some poor hen gets well shampooed despite her frantic cries.
You come with us to breakfast and share the toast and tea
And then you help to make the beds and wash the crocks with me.
And when it comes to ten o'clock we have to say goodbye,
But not without a sense of loss and not without a sigh.

After many years of listening to your program I have the urge to put pen to paper. Listening to *Australia All Over* on Sunday morning recently I heard you make a statement that there are no giveaways on your program. I beg to differ. *Australia All Over* has more giveaways than any other radio station in Australia.

The pleasure, humour, enjoyment and nostalgia that is passed out on that special Sunday morning each week is more than evident from what we hear of other people's letters to the program.

Keep up the good work. My wife is still in shock as this is the longest letter I have written in thirty-five years of married bliss!

It was great to hear you so clearly via 3LO for that couple of Sundays, although I must say it fair threw out our Sunday routine of scrabbling around the dial for ages trying to find you amidst the static and whining that seems to be the best we can hope for on the regionals. It would be a great PR exercise for the Ibeysea (ABC!) to put you back on 3LO. So many city folk listen to you under what can only be deemed extreme conditions—a sure indicator of the popularity of Oz-All-Over.

My Dad put us onto Oz-All-Over. He listens to you religiously—he doesn't go to church though—and whenever we go up to stay with them (at Edi, a glorious little spot outside Wangaratta) the Sunday ritual has become tea and toast in the big bed in Mum and Dad's room listening to you.

Because of this newest family tradition I've learnt a great deal of new things about my folks—not so much about the old days, when Dad drove sheep in outback Queensland or Mum worked in her Dad's eucy. factory in Kingower—we know about that—but about what makes them tick. Things like how they have a deep, abiding antipathy for the Japanese (it's hatred actually, but I find that difficult to say) and yet Mum can't sing along to 'Sayonara Nakimura' because she cries a little each time. And how my Dad calls Aborigines 'boongs' (even though some were his mates) but thinks what you and Ted Egan and Oodjeroo Noonuccle have to say is 'bloody right—y'know'. I watch him now, after one of you have had your say, and see him mulling over your words and wrestling with his thoughts, and he'll say something quite positive. I've come to realise a lot of what he has had to say through the years is the result of the peer pressure of the bushies he has been one of and lived with for so long; all he's really needed was the other side of the story to balance things. That you and your program have given him that is one of the wonderful things in life. It has also developed in me a deeper respect for my parents, helped me understand them better and be more patient with their opinions. It cuts both ways too: I've noticed my Dad, especially, listens to me more now and doesn't get that look on his face which indicated to me he thought I was just another one of those mad greenies (and Uni. student to boot) who had nothing better to do than stir the possum.

Your few hours each Sunday has opened up an avenue of communication, tolerance and understanding that just might have remained closed-off for us, and that's another of the wonderful things in life.

WARS & ANZAC DAY

When I first heard Kevin Baker's 'The Snowy River Men' I was almost moved to tears. Such a powerful song, it expresses all the things we feel about war and its futility. It remains one of my favourite songs.

In 1992 especially, because of the fifty-year anniversaries of the Battle of the Coral Sea and the bombing of Darwin and so on, we've had a lot of letters about war, and I still get letters and poems about great-uncles and grandfathers in World War I. There's no shortage of those memories: Australians seem to have a great penchant for fighting in other people's wars.

A Golden Day

Discussion about wattle on recent programs reminded me that at this time of the year I often think of the day that was one of the highlights of my childhood. It was the day World War II ended, 15 August, 1945.

At that time I was a ten-year-old schoolgirl living at Cowra in central New South Wales. We knew the war was ending and there was much discussion of it at school. If the Japanese signed the surrender the war would be over and there would be a two-day holiday.

As it happened, our school's athletics carnival was planned for 15 August, but if the war ended there would be no carnival that day. Instead, the school would take part in a march through the town. I hoped fervently that the war would end because I hated athletics carnivals! A march and a holiday would be much more fun than running around at the dusty, windy oval.

We had been told we didn't have to come to school until after the Prime Minister's broadcast, scheduled for 9.30 am. I remember sitting on the floor in front of my father's large wooden wireless set, waiting for the speech. That day the wireless was turned on early, as there was usually a time of static and whistles while the wireless 'warmed up'. There must have been great rejoicing in every home in Australia when the announcement was made that the war in the Pacific had ended. I went off to school, thrilled at the thought of not having to go to a sports carnival.

That afternoon the whole town turned out for a march through the streets. There were soldiers from Cowra's two army camps, children from all the schools, Land Army girls, women in Red Cross uniform. There was music from the military band, the Salvation Army band and the town band. As an added touch of cheerfulness the members of the town band wore sprigs of wattle in their caps.

After the march the band played dance music and people danced in the main street. My father, who sternly disapproved of dancing, said nothing against this. He must have felt that it was appropriate for the occasion.

The wattle in the musicians' caps was a nice touch as Cowra had many wattle trees, both in town and on the hillsides, and at this time of year they were all in bloom.

I remember this exciting day as a golden day in my childhood.

FROM: WINSOME SMITH, Baulkham Hills, NSW

I heard you play 'G'Day, G'Day' and thought you might be interested in the following.

I left for Turkey on a charter tour by the RSL and Torchbearers to attend the commemoration of the Anzac Landing. My husband was at the landing and it was a special event for me. We had a sixteen-day tour of Turkey, and one of our group gave the coach driver a tape of 'G'day, G'day'. The driver spoke no English but fell in love with the recording. I know it is a fun song, but can you imagine sixteen days listening to it!

The Anzac service was a wonderful though very sad experience for me. At eighty-six it took a lot of determination to make the pilgrimage but it was so worthwhile. It was amazing how the veterans aged from 92 to 103 stood up to the trauma of the return.

I have a particular interest in the Kalumburu Mission and it's people who, of course, rescued those 120 souls from the SS *Koolama* when it was bombed.

During the 1939–45 war I was a radar mechanic in the RAAF, and for the last year of the war was stationed on Sir Graham Moore Island. This island is just off the coast of the north-eastern corner of Western Australia. Hence it is not far from Kalumburu Mission, about thirty nautical miles. The monks were frequent visitors to the island, sailing across in their very old lugger to say Mass for us and to offer whatever help, spiritual or otherwise, was appropriate.

In July 1990 I was fortunate to be able to realise an ambition and return to the island. I stayed at the Mission and learnt about the amazing contribution to the 1939-45 war effort made by the monks. The *Koolama* incident was just one of a number of episodes. Unfortunately, none of this has been recorded anywhere but remains only in the memories of those who were involved.

I made up my mind to do something about it. When I returned home I approached the members of the Victorian RAAF Radar Association. The result is that we now have a bronze plaque which details the whole story. It is presently in my possession but will soon be sent off to Kalumburu for mounting in the Mission grounds.

Incidentally, these are the same people who rescued the two German aviators, Bertram and Klausman, who crashed at Cape Bernier in 1932. Cape Bernier is only about thirty kilometres south-east of Leseur Island, where ten years later the *Koolama* was bombed. Following the rescue of Bertram and Klausman,the German Ambassador in Australia in appreciation presented to the Mission a church organ. Unfortunately, this organ was damaged when the Japanese bombed the Mission on

FROM:
WARWICK BUTLER
Brisbane, Queensland

27 September 1943. The organ is now on display in the museum at the Benedictine Monastery at New Norcia in West Australia.

Here is a poem of Dad's which may be appropriate for Anzac Day:

Dad was a POW of the Japanese for three-and-a-half years and spent a good deal of that time on the infamous railway line. Thus the inspiration to write 'Mates'.

Mates

I've travelled down some lonely roads,
Both crooked tracks and straight,
An' I 'ave learned life's noblest creed
Summed up in one word . . . 'Mate'.

I'm thinkin' back across the years,
(A thing I do of late)
An' this word sticks between me ears:
'You've got to 'ave a mate'.

Me mind goes back to '43,
To slavery an' 'ate,
When man's one chance to stay alive
Depended on 'is mate.

With bamboo for a billy-can
An' bamboo for a plate,
A bamboo paradise for bugs
Was bed for me and mate.

You'd slip an' slither through the mud
An' curse your rotten fate;
But then you'd 'ear a quiet word:
'Don't drop your bundle, mate'.

An' though it's all so long ago,
This truth I 'ave to state:
A man don't know what 'lonely' means
'Til 'e 'as lost 'is mate.

If there's a life that follers this,
If there's a 'Golden Gate',
The welcome that I want to 'ear
Is just: 'Good on y' mate'.

An' so to all who ask us why
We keep these special dates
Like Anzac Day, I answer: 'Why?
We're thinkin' of our mates'.

An' when I've left the driver's seat
An' 'anded in me plates,
I'll tell 'ol Peter at the door:
'I've come to join me mates'.

I was prompted to write after hearing 'The Snowy River Men'. My interest in this brilliant portrayal of the trauma of war set to music relates to me being a son-in-law of one of Leslie Allen's younger brothers.

Perhaps two or three years ago you passed a comment about 'Woolumba', NSW, wondering who lived there. Well, the Allen family dairied there and, after being burnt out by bush fires, moved to Bibbenluke on the Monaro. Leslie was teaching school there on the 10th January 1916 when the Snowy River March, which commenced in Delegate, passed through Bibbenluke on its way to Goulburn and he was one of four members of that community who 'signed their names right down' and failed to return from that war.

Leslie was a member of the 55th Battalion. He died of wounds on 19th May, 1916 and is buried in the British cemetery at Grevilliers near Arras in France. I was fortunate enough to have been a member of the RSL group that visited Gallipoli for the 75th Anniversary and then toured the battlefields of France. On the last day of our twenty-three day tour I was able to visit Leslie's grave, perhaps his only visitor in seventy-four years. When we left the cemetery at Grevilliers I was able to have the song 'Snowy River Men', played over the PA on our coach to the very attentive members of our party. It portrayed very graphically the story of just one of those hundreds of thousands of graves so neatly tended in France today.

Do you know there is a one-room school house not more than ten miles from the Sydney GPO? Yes, you will find it at Oxford Falls, five hundred yards off the Wakehurst Parkway. Oxford Falls consists of no more than twenty little farms that produce pigs, poultry, fruit, flowers, vegies and honey, which is mostly sold on two roadside stalls, a telephone box, a couple of houses, a wee church and a school.

The school is surrounded by bush and consists of the school house, a shelter shed, toilets of course, a flag pole, a quadrangle, and a little war memorial. Once a year the little school excels itself, and that is when it has its Anzac Day dawn parade. It is a simple ceremony. The muffled drum, the shuffling feet, the lone bugler, the address by a prominent citizen, and then three hundred or more voices sing a hymn that will ring out across the valley in the amazing stillness of the early morning.

FROM:
PETER PINNEY
Wilston
Queensland

There's an unusual happening about to take place here in Brisbane—a real Boree Log affair, with a hundred old warriors travelling in from Australia all over, literally.

The survivors of an Australian Commando Squadron who fought in World War II are having their first reunion in forty five years. Their first reunion, and their last—there'll never be another.

I think every army unit has a bit of a get together every now and then, but with the commandos there was always a problem. They weren't recruited from any particular section of the nation: they were selected from established army units, and this means, like I said, that they came from all over Australia.

The logistics of getting them all together for a ding were a bit daunting: but suddenly, after all these years, when one-third of us are still alive it's all happening.

The Sixth Royal Australian Regiment has offered to host the reunion here at Enoggera Army Barracks over five days and nights during Anzac Week—army tucker at cost and free tent accommodation. The RAAF is bringing blokes from thousands of miles away by regular Hercules. A Bundaberg firm is providing medicinal rum, and Carlton's are donating sundry kegs in case anyone happens to raise a thirst telling lies about the battles they all won. This is going to be the mother of all reunions!

Not that there were any battles won, really. The role of the 2/8th Commando Squadron in World War II was to hit the Japanese where least expected and shoot through; to collect information, to sabotage and burn and harass—the usual tactics of any guerilla mob. On Bougainville they operated for ten months well behind the enemy lines, plucking prisoners as required and ambushing enemy roads, busting things, making lightning attacks on strongpoints and racing off into the mulga before things got dangerous. The ideal way to fight. Very few commandos were killed. But no big victories, no captured cities or second fronts. Small beans, really.

And now they're all going to meet again, after nearly half a century. A problem, though: when they all gather at Enoggera Army Barracks on this April 23, each man will be looking for the lean, hard striplings who were their mates so long ago, and all they'll see is a bunch of old geezers all bulging in the wrong places and sagging at the seams.

But for anyone watching us march on Anzac Day, proud behind that bold Commando banner, well, there'll be no sadness then. Or at the farewell dinner, even though, with all of us now nudging seventy and eighty years, we'll never meet again.

Do you know Australia's greatest day? It was 8th August, 1918. It will be the 73rd anniversary of the day that five divisions of Diggers went over the top on a twenty mile point from Villiers-Brett to Amiens and annihilated Germany's six best divisions. We broke the might, the back and the heart of the German Army that day. We advanced ten miles, took thousands of German prisoners and never stopped advancing till the war was over. We went through the Hindenberg Line and took the big gun that those Germans had been shelling Paris with for two years.

See, the going was tough. We took the places called Mont St Quenton, Penonne, etc., got those Germans on the run and kept them on the run. Don't take my word for this. General Ludendorf in his memoirs after the war said 'We lost the war on 8th August 1918 on a twenty mile point between Amiens and Villiers-Brett'. They knew the Aussies were there and they knew we had five divisions, so they put in their six best divisions to stop our five.

MAGIC IN THE TENT

We had a great time in Toowoomba doing an outside broadcast. Lynn Hopkins, of Gordonvale, was there in the tent along with a thousand or so other people; she had such a good time she burst into verse:

It was countdown of the hours for the Carnival of Flowers
With cornbeef, mince and even drover's stew
When we eyed off the place and quickened our pace
To see Ian in the tent with you know who.

In the early morning light towards the end of night
The campfires in Queens Park were burning brightly
With the billy on the boil and the boys hard at their toil
Serving breakfast to the faithful stepping spritely.

He played the song 'G'day', had an interview with Kay
And talked about the ring road with the mayor
And by the time he crossed for news and other people's views
Everyone was scrambling for a chair.

The day was heaven sent and it was magic in the tent
And things could not have progressed any finer
With some live calls on the line and the weather forecast fine
And a comment from the local water diviner.

The bloke got off his mount as he gave his last head count
As Ian cast his eyes around the crowd
And the songs from Bandy Bill gave us Aussies quite a thrill
And gave us every reason to be proud.

The pioneers, you see, were the Durack family
With O'Briens from Defiance came along
There was magic in the tent but at 10 am it went
As 'Macca' closed his show down with a song.

FROM OVERSEAS

Dick Smith, Resolute, Alaska USA 3 May 1987

Ian Gill, Camp Davies, Antarctica 8 May 1988

Jock Schmeisshen, Casey Station, Antarctica,
    1 February 1989

Barbara Erskine, Ottowa, Canada 12 February 1989

George Merriman, Rabaul, PNG 26 March 1989

Ron Heeney, Timaru, New Zealand 7 May 1989

Scott Darling, Eugene, Oregon USA 25 June 1989

David Woodhouse, Ambon Harbour, Indonesia 30 July 1989

Elizabeth Durack, Galway, Ireland 1 October 1989

Catherine Phillips, Auckland, New Zealand
    10 December 1989

Morris Stewart, Tabubil, PNG 11 February 1990

Norm Sheridan, Coconut Island 25 February 1990

Bill Jarmin, Cocos Island 11 March 1990

Phil Histek, San Francisco USA 18 March 1990

Pam Cupper, Turkey 22 April 1990

Tim Fischer MP, Athens, Greece 22 April 1990

Mike, Honiara, Solomon Islands 20 May 1990

Dominic Spora, Ireland 15 July 1990

Tom Reiser, Chicago USA 12 August 1990

Shane Hughes, Raritonga, Cook Islands 12 May 1991

Lt Col Terry Boyce, Vanimo, PNG 19 May 1991

Tim Fischer MP, Crete 26 May 1991

Peter Shaw, Kitchener, Ontario, Canada 21 July 1991

Margaret Smee, Futomi, Japan 20 October 1991

David Rand, Coconut Island 17 November 1991

Jason Roberts, Spitzbergen, Near North Pole
    17 November 1991

Margaret Morgan, Hampshire, England 1 December 1991

Paul Conroy, Japan 5 April 1992

Jo Irwin, New York USA 31 May 1992

Mieke Burns, The Netherlands 26 July 1992

FROM PLANES

Geoff Kendall, en route to Thursday Island, near Lizard
    Island 6 January 1988

Rod Harmer, Ansett en route to Adelaide 11 June 1989

Warwick Tainton Qantas flight to Brisbane 13 August 1989

John Salmon, fish spotter off Tasmania

Dr Bob Balmain, RFDS, near Charleville 28 June 1992

FROM BOATS AND SHIPS

Kathy, *Verbatim*, round Australia race 25 September, 9
    October, 16 October, 1987, 6 January 1988

Richard Ferguson, *Lady Franklin*, Antarctica
    6 November 1988

Bill Young, *Shell Five*, off Weipa 15 October 1989

Ken Hinchliff, *Iron Capricorn*, 22 January 1989

Crew on *Rig Seismic*, off Victorian coast, 26 March 1989

Eddie Newman, off Port Davey, Tasmania 3 September 1989

Robert Owen, *Bounty*, off Coffs Harbour 3 June 1990

Bradley Hogan, *Byron Star* prawn trawler, Spencer Gulf
    29 October 1989

Ian Gibson, *Balac-Papan*, near Thursday Island
    11 February 1990

Bob Ellis, *Elizabeth EII*, Moore Reef, Coral Sea 8 July 1990

David Beard, *Scaffy* off Wessell Island 12 August 1990

Nigel Scullion, *Kalidris*, north of Melville Island 21 April 1991

Mike Kellaher, *New Horizons*, near Crescent Head
    4 August 1991

Purser David Walton, *One and All*, near Brisbane
    18 August 1991

Bob Harris, *Ironbark II*, 200 miles off Gold Coast
    27 October 1991

Ronnie, Indian Coal Ship, in the Whitsundays
    26 January 1992

Captain Geoff Walpole, HMAS *Perth*, Jakarta, Indonesia

Captain Rob Ray, Tug *Aggressor*, off Hong Kong
    19 April 1992

Roy Lewisson, *Tysay*, mid-Atlantic, between Spain and
    N. America

Captain John Lord, HMAS *Hobart*, off San Diego USA

Tonya Roberts, *Young Endeavour* New York, 5 July 1992

FROM ISLANDS

Brian McGurgan, Willis Island, 17 May 1987

Phil Vaughan, Fitzroy Island, Lighthouse 16 August 1987

Marcus Tilley, Norfolk Island, 6 March 1988

Warren Hand, Thursday Island, 18 September 1988

Ron Owens, Lord Howe Island, 4 December 1988

David Cinzio, Neptune Island, 11 December 1988

Darryl Binns, Macquarie Island, 15 January 1989

Ken Goodman, Lamb Island, 22 January 1989

John Riordan, Partridge Island, 29 January 1989

Frank Wright, Russell Island, 5 February 1989

Beth Fitzharding, Abrolhos Island, 16 April 1989

Mark Hall, Heron Island Research Station 21 May 1989

Tex Battle, Swears Island, 28 May 1989

Kay Keller, Moa Island, 11 June 1989

Dave & Maxine Maxwell, Hindmarsh Island,
    26 November 1989

Dixie Lambert, Stradbroke Island, 25 February 1990

John O'Sullivan, Melville Island, 8 July 1990

Bill Cloyne, Kangaroo Island, 12 August 1990

Tanya Sunstrup, Swan Island, 16 December 1990

Helen Bankshell, Coolan Island, 4 August 1991

Shirley, Bribie Island, 18 August 1991

Les, Boyne Island, 3 November 1991

John Hickling, Middle Percy Island, 1 December 1991

Steve, Groote Eylandt, 1 December 1991

Grant, Norfolk Island, 8 March 1992

Mark, Preservation Island, 22 March 1992

Peg, Phillip Island, 29 March 1992

TREES

What great letters are in this section on trees—about pepper trees and gum trees. Of course, this is only a small sample of the marvellous letters that I receive and don't get time to read on the program. The letters to *Australia All Over* and the material for the rest of the program are kept on file in our office. It really all needs to be catalogued properly as a repository of Australian social history.

Speaking of trees, there's a wonderful tree near where I live. It's a Sydney red gum. I think it's an angophora, not strictly a eucalyptus, although I'm not an expert. It's a beautiful tree and I wouldn't like to hazard a guess as to how old it is. Sometimes I lean against it, looking up into its branches. It's like looking at the stars, and my mind starts to wonder about all sorts of things.

Sticks

When I was a child I had to get the morning wood. I remember my mother asking, 'Have you got the morning sticks?'

I used to enjoy getting them and took pride in doing it correctly as I was taught at an early age. I loved the smell of the broken sticks and their burning aroma, too. I used to hunt around in the grass, choosing the size needed—some thin, some thick, some with leaves still on. I learnt how to place them on my arm so they wouldn't fall—a few bigger ones first, the smallest last. I knew where to place my foot on the branch so that when I broke it a piece wouldn't fly up and hit me. I learnt just what was needed to get a fire going quickly in the morning. By the time Dad carried in the bucket of fresh milk the kettle was boiling on the stove.

What would we do without sticks? We use them all the time. We use them to draw mud maps in the dirt and to stake plants. I always keep a stack of sticks under the tankstand for a rainy day.

We have planted hundreds of trees on our farm, so there will be plenty of sticks in the futue, as well as hollows for the birds, leaves for koalas and nectar for the bees and honey-eaters.

Give a Tree a Hug

I was havin' a yarn with a spotted gum
Me arms wrapped round its trunk,
When a voice called out from up the track
'Are you crook, or flamin' drunk?'
'No,' I replied, 'nothin' wrong,
I do this once in a while—
Haven't you ever hugged a tree
And seen it's branches smile?

'Haven't you felt the lively warmth
And then almost in a trance
Looked up to hear it talkin' back
With the leaves on the breeze at a dance?'
"No, of course not,' the stranger said,
'I'm a man, not a flamin' kid!'
He then walked off without a word
Not stoppin' to dip his lid.

So I finished yarnin' with the gum
Once more to be on me way,
Admirin' the beauty of the bush
And the bonza sunny day;
But then I stopped in some surprise
And gave a happy shrug
For the stranger up in the distance
Was givin' a tree a hug!

FROM:
ALLAN B. R.
HARVEY

TREES

About eight years ago I attended the Lizard Races at Eulo, about fifty miles west of Cunnamulla. Quite an interesting event. It is held fairly close to the only hotel in that area, the Eulo Queen. The proceeds all go to the Flying Doctors Fund.

A barbeque was in progress and you could hardly see the ladies serving or the men cooking for the myriad of bush flies whirling about. John Payne and I got a hamburger each and I said to him, 'Let's get under the pepper trees.' He queried, 'Why?' I said, 'You'll see.' As soon as we moved under the pepper trees, no flies at all! Still millions outside, so I think that's why the pepper trees were planted.

I would like to tell you about a beautiful avenue of pepper trees that lead to the homestead station of 'Glenroc', seventeen miles out of Gunnedah, NSW.

My father planted these trees in the late 1950s. They were only tiny but I can still remember him with two buckets of water, walking up to the gate and giving each of them a little water each day or so. The trees are big now and a lovely green and whenever I see them I think of the care my father gave them. Dad has been gone nearly twenty years and my brother runs the property now, but the pepper trees will always be there, or at least for many years.

P.S. We were on Perigian Beach when the whale was pulled out to sea. There wasn't a dry eye on the beach.

In February 1942 about forty primary school girls from Brighton College, Manly, were evacuated to a vacated station homestead, 'Dalkeith', on the railway line three miles north of Gundagai. I was one of them and our average age was eight. We were city kids, the majority of us homesick and frightened. We saw troop trains going by and waved our towels at them. We watched the skies for enemy planes, and I recall we were all lined up and told of the Coral Sea victory.

Our news, in the form of letters, came with Mr Jeremiah, in his open car. He was disabled so could not join up. He was the only man we saw and he was our link with our families who tried to keep our spirits up with news of loved ones and pets. We were not so considerate. We knew our letters were censored but we continued to write about the drought, dead sheep, bush fires, drowned flies in our food, sour milk, castor oil and our weekly bath. (We lined up on Saturdays and shared the bath water.) We also gave them weekly bulletins on the slow, progressive death of the twenty-four chooks brought to provide us with eggs.

There was a pepper tree in the chook run but my pepper tree was outside my dormitory—ten beds were crammed into what would have been the homestead dining room. I took my letters to read under its branches, I hid in it to escape from the school bully. My friends and I swung from it, we made a cubby house in its shade, and whispered escape plans behind it. I can still recall the perfume of its leaves, specially when I shed my tears there. This tree is my lingering memory of a difficult, but worthwhile, period of adjustment in my early life. I wonder if it is still there?

FROM:
DAVID SEARLE
Taperoo
South Australia

I have seen peppercorn trees growing in many places, but I was very surprised to see them growing at a railway settlement on the Nullabor Plain. I had been under the impression that large trees could not be grown on the Nullabor.

These trees were really big and very healthy, too. They were probably well cared for and watered in their seedling days, but I doubt whether they were being watered at the time when I saw them because they would have needed huge amounts of water, and water is not plentiful in that particular place.

Seeing the peppercorns made me wonder if any large gums or wattles could be grown on the Nullabor if they were cared for when planted as seedlings.

FROM:
DOUG & SHIRLEY
STEVENSON
Bairnsdale
Victoria

The segment on peppercorn trees, while informative and botanically authoritative, failed to mention two very significant features of peppercorns, or at least significant to a generation of young boys and girls in Victoria.

1 Peppercorn trees are a favoured site for Gum Emperor moths to lay their eggs. Many a youngster in the 1940s and 50s spent a lot of time searching peppercorn trees for the eggs or caterpillars of this large moth. These were taken home and kept in a shoe or butter box, much to the despair of long suffering mums, and fed at regular intervals with fresh peppercorn foliage. Eventually the large, green, colourful caterpillars would spin their cocoons. Generally they were forgotten about at this stage, and many cocoons would be thrown away in the room tidying process. But the family would often be reminded of the caterpillar season at a later stage when the appearance of a large moth in the kitchen or living room heralded the emergence of this magnificent moth from its hard, brown cocoon.

2 In the same era that I am referring to it was customary for primary

school boys and girls to periodically arm themselves with 'pea-shooters', a toy or harmless version of the blowpipe. The favourite ammunition for these terrors of the schoolroom or playground was the large immature fruit of the peppercorn. They were somewhat bitter to keep in your mouth, but any self-respecting pea-shooter exponent happily suffered this discomfort for the sake of using such good ear-stinging projectiles.

Every time the subject of pepper trees is raised on your program I feel sure someone will point out that probably the most important feature of this tree is its ability to grow in stockyards.

It is one of the few trees capable of growing in the high-manure content levels of these areas! One has only to note the number of pepper trees which have been planted in country saleyards, providing much needed shade for both man and beast, to realise this.

I wanted to tell you about my pepper tree. It is outside my kitchen window, far away enough not to be a danger to any drainage and foundations.

It was planted in 1909, and is a huge tree, twenty-three feet around its girth. I'm afraid I am having a bit of the same problem as I get older!

It has acted as my cow bale over the years, doesn't keep out the wind and the rain, but keeps me in the shade in the hot summer months.

While milking my cow, I had a regular visitor, Harry the cat, who came for his milkshake every morning. Harry has since passed away. He would push up against me until I squirted milk into his mouth, and if I ignored him his foot would come up and he would tap me constantly.

The pepper tree has been trimmed by the chainsaw, kept levelled by the sheep, rubbed on by the cattle and is still thriving. It's a wonderful sight in the early mornings to look out my kitchen window and see the sun just coming up behind it.

Last week a woman mentioned the pepper trees which used to be so much a part of the country scene, especially around the farmhouse.

They're a hardy tree, and often the only thing left in the garden around ruined farms. When I visit such ruins and see the rings of stones where the hard-won flower gardens used to be, or sit in the shade of the pepper tree regarding the tumbled stonework, I often wonder about the people who lived there. The piles of broken glass and crockery set me thinking about unknown details of their lives. Who broke that bowl with the willow pattern—was it a child, and if so, how much trouble did that child get into over it? Who slept in the old iron framed double bed—how many babies were conceived and born in it, and how many folk breathed their last in it? Were the people who lived in this house happy? What were their lives like? Where are their descendants now?

The pepper trees they planted are a living reminder of those pioneering days, yet are rarely seen nowadays, apart from close to old homesteads and ruins. They're an attractive tree, fast-growing, drought and frost resistant, with a drooping willowy form and tiny red (I believe edible) berries. I understand they were so named (pepper trees) as the berries were ground as a pepper substitute.

I wanted to share with you my joy and constant rediscovery of my deep love and respect for the Australian bush, in particular the gums.

They have the power to clear the cobwebs of sadness or confusion. They stand like true, beautiful friends, there for you in their silvery goodness, strong, clear, wise and patient.

I've felt for a long time that their form is so clearly linked to the human form. They wrinkle and gently curve whenever a new direction needs to be taken. Looking at the scars and bumps that these new directions have left is like looking at a person, old or young. We can only guess what personal weather charts lie hidden behind the present forms.

The wattle, and other fragrances there, possess their own gifts of nourishment as well. I feel now that the act of breathing in the bush air is like drinking a golden elixir, full of goodness and a myriad other life-giving qualities.

I find it very exciting that we are at last beginning to show some wisdom by honouring indigenous people's methods of healing. Australian bush flower remedies are wonderful. When we marry the best of theirs and ours it will be like receiving a bottle of some magnificent elixir, the price of which will be respect and patience and the ability to really use our eyes for seeing and our ears for listening. All bound up with understanding hearts.

Although this wild wind we've been having brings some restless nights, it also brings an abundant supply of firewood. A couple of weeks ago, early one Sunday morning, I drove to a favourite spot to walk my dog and collect some fuel for the fire. Being early and a bit chilly, I was wondering whether or not I really wanted to be there or back home in bed. There's quite a lot of wattle out in bloom right now, and when I stopped my little truck and opened the door the gently caressing smell of those little golden flowers soon dispelled any notion of bed. I'm constantly amazed at how nurturing they are, like the voice of a wise and caring old woman.

Most of the sticks I collected were quite long and I initially thought that I'd simply throw them in the back and break them up when I got home. I was so honoured when I changed my mind and decided to break the first few up then and there, alone among the gum trees. The sound of their snapping rang through the bush and brought some early memories rushing back to me, and yet at the same time I experienced the beauty of clear simplicity.

I heard your interesting piece on river red gums. This reminded me of some verses I wrote fifty-five years ago when, as a homesick Australian adolescent, I had entered the cloistered life of a girls' English boarding school. The fate of the red gums at that time in the south-east of South Australia is self-evident. The verses appeared in the school magazine.

FROM:
ALISON WELBOURN
Glenalta, South Australia

The Old Gum Tree

The old gum tree
Stands quite alone—
Quite alone in the grass knee-deep,
While in his shade the silent sheep
Lay themselves down in peaceful sleep.

The old gum tree!
His ancient boughs,
Knotted and gnarled in ancient state,
Year in, year out, await their fate,
For ring-barkers working early and late.

On this gum tree
The beautiful leaves
Toss and sway in the perfumed breeze,
While sleepy parrots and laden bees
Stop to rest in this tree of trees.

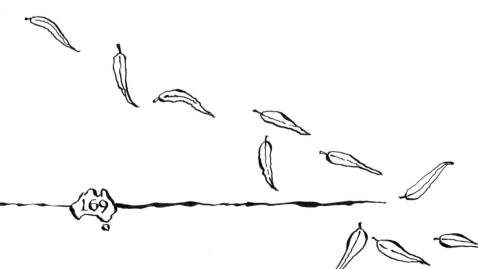

Australia All Over

I haven't seen Australia
All over, well not yet,
I am not sure how far
My man and I will get,
But though I cannot see it,
It is a certain bet
That I can still explore it,
Via my radio set.

For every Sunday morning,
Macca's cheery tone
Wakes me from my dreaming
In my bed at home.
He roams the whole land over,
With people on the phone;
With Macca on the air-waves
One cannot feel alone.

From Hobart up to Darwin,
From Sydney to the West,
Macca takes us all around,
With every phone-in guest.
And it is an exciting
And int'resting talk-fest;
In showing us around our land
Macca is the best.

I haven't seen Australia
All over, but I know
All the things that one should see,
The places one should go.
I may not see Australia,
The lot, from go to whoa;
But I can learn about it
Each week, on Macca's show.

FROM: HELEN BRUMBY, Rose Bay, Tasmania